Straight Talk about Investing for Your Retirement

Other *Straight Talk* Books from McGraw-Hill

Straight Talk about Investing for Your Retirement

Dian Vujovich

McGraw-Hill, Inc.

New York   San Francisco   Washington, D.C.   Auckland   Bogotá
Caracas   Lisbon   London   Madrid   Mexico City   Milan
Montreal   New Delhi   San Juan   Singapore
Sydney   Tokyo   Toronto

Library of Congress Cataloging-in-Publication Data

Vujovich, Dian.
    Straight talk about investing for your retirement / Dian Vujovich.
        p.   cm.
    Includes index.
    ISBN 0-07-067010-2
    1. Investments—United States. 2. Retirement—Planning.
  I. Title.
  HG4921.V84   1995
  332.6—dc20
                                    95-10018
                                       CIP

1 2 3 4 5 6 7 8 9 0 DOC/DOC 9 0 0 9 8 7 6 5

ISBN 0-07-067010-2

The sponsoring editor for this book was Betsy Brown, the editing supervisor was Jane Palmieri, and the production supervisor was Donald Schmidt. It was set in Palatino by Victoria Khavkina of McGraw-Hill's Professional Book Group composition unit.

Printed and bound by R. R. Donnelley & Sons Company.

This book is dedicated to each and every one of us who needs to be reminded of how vitally important it is to save money for our upcoming retirement years.

Contents

Introduction

If there is ever a time when continuing education is all important, it happens when each of us faces the financial issues of retirement—that stage in life when the pressures of the workplace and money making are supposed to be behind us and life is to be leisurely enjoyed.

But knowing how to save and invest for retirement isn't something we've been taught much about and therefore isn't necessarily a top priority in our lives. Unfortunately, not being financially prepared for retirement means that the dreams we may have of spending those nonworking days lollygagging on the beach, playing endless rounds of golf, traveling the world, or visiting the grandchildren might not come true.

When I first began doing research for this book, I didn't know how very important creating a retirement savings plan was for each one of us; how ill prepared most of us are when it comes to planning for our retirement years; and how difficult it is to get straight talk about retirement investing ideas, products, or plans.

All of us, it seems, have our own ideas about where we will get the money to be able to afford retirement, but not all of those ideas are followed through with sound actions. From the financial decision maker in your household who says that he will begin saving for retirement after the kids are out of school, after the house is paid for, or after whatever, to the person selling investment products for retirement, to the employer who either offers no retirement plans for her employees or, if she does, forgets to take the time to inform and educate her workers as to the ins and outs of long-term retirement planning, the devil in the "are-you-actively-preparing-for-your-retirement?" mirror can as easily be a reflection of ourself as it is anyone else.

Along with everything else, retirement is also a subject that is real easy to avoid, particularly when you're young. When I was in my twenties and thirties, for instance, it was a subject I tried to avoid and even feared. I feared it basically because I didn't know how to deal with it. And not knowing how to deal with it made me feel isolated, as though I was probably the only person in the country who didn't have a well-thought-out and well-executed retirement plan in place for myself. Boy, was I ever wrong!

All it took was a few phone calls to friends and acquaintances, and brief interviews with professional associates, to realize that there are many people in their thirties and forties—and even fifties and sixties—who have done very little retirement planning.

Even people who are employees of companies in which retirement plans and programs are a part of their benefits packages more often than not know very little about the ins and outs of the plans offered them.

For the self-employed, those between jobs, or those holding low- to moderate-paying jobs, the situation is frequently worse; personal retirement planning isn't dealt with because it's often unaffordable. I can't tell you the number of people I have spoken with who have said quite candidly, "I don't have the money to save for my retirement because I live from paycheck to paycheck."

But with money or without, finding a way to save for your retirement is as essential in today's world as having the money to pay your phone or power bill and rent or mortgage. Why? Because living, at whatever age or stage in life, costs money. Period. And living in retirement can easily cost as much—if not more—than what life costs during the decades before it.

When considering the cost of living during those golden years include these facts: currently only about one-half of the employed take advantage of the retirement plans their employers provide them; Social Security, some speculate, will be broke by the year 2029; and because of longer life expectancies, the years spent in retirement could be very financially compromising unless you personally save money for them.

Straight Talk about Investing for Your Retirement is a primer book about retirement planning. In it you will learn why it is so important to save for your upcoming retirement years and how, by saving or investing just a few dollars a month, you can begin to build a nest egg independent of what Social Security, your company's retirement plans, or an inheritance might provide. You'll also be introduced to the jargon of the retirement industry along with some of the common types of retirement investment products that people often choose when salting away money for their retirement years. And you'll find some long-term investing ideas; questions to ask your employer about the retirement plans offered; questions to ask yourself about your current retirement holdings; and checklists to help you understand the investments you make before you buy them.

Although I searched for some formula, some magic answer, some one-size-fits-all response to the two-part question, How much money will I need to retire, and how will I get it? the truth of the matter is that there isn't one. The answers to each part of that question are different for every single one of us.

Knowing then that the only person who can really come up with the amount of savings you'll need to accumulate for retirement is you, and that accumulating that money depends upon the kinds of savings and investment choices you make, it pays to learn as much as possible about the subject.

No longer are the simple skills of reading, writing, and 'rithmatic enough to carry us along in life. Today we all must enthusiastically embrace the added skill of money management if we want to live comfortably during our retiring decades. It is my hope that *Straight Talk about Investing for Your Retirement* will help you on the learning road to long-term money management. And from it you'll take away some tools that will help you create a nest egg that makes your retirement a financially comfortable one.

Good luck, and I'll see you in your seventies. I'll be the one sipping piña coladas in the cabana right next to yours on the beach in Hawaii.

Acknowledgments

One of my favorite words is *grateful*. It's a word that summons up all kinds of feelings of thankfulness inside of me and serves as a reminder that while I may indeed be the author of this book, putting it together took the talents, skills, minds, and help of many, many others.

With that sense of I-couldn't-have-done-it-without-you, I would like to thank my editors for their direction and patience in this project and the friendships and professional guidance of a whole host of other people including Nancy Mlinarchik, Ray Hess, Joan and John Howley, Drew Bottaro, Dee Lee, Wayne Smith, Elizabeth Usovicz, and Bill Broughton along with the dozens of others who listened, suggested, and wondered if I'd ever finish this book before it was time for me to retire.

Dian Vujovich

PART 1

How Much Do You Know about Retirement?

1
Facing
the Facts

*I have enough money to last me the rest of my
life, unless I buy something.*

JACKIE MASON

There's a crisis coming your way. One you can avoid. Or one that will smack you right across the face if you choose to ignore it. That crisis centers around your retirement. And it focuses on the question, "Where will I get the money to be able to retire?"

Having money during your retirement—whether those years are ahead of you or part of your life already—is a financial responsibility resting squarely upon your own shoulders. It's not the government's, or your employer's, or the lottery official in your home state's responsibility to ensure that you've accumulated enough retirement income and savings to get you and your loved ones through your golden years—it's yours. And if there is a personal state of emergency facing the majority of Americans today, it concerns how poorly most people have planned for their retirement—a retirement that can easily last 10, 20, 30, or even 40 years. Or roughly one-quarter to one-third of a person's entire life!

The underlying reason for this impending crisis isn't because of interest rates or the stock market. Nor is it because of Democrats or Republicans. The reason is simple: We are living longer lives today than we ever have before in our recorded history, and we're not planning for them financially. There are no ifs, ands, or buts about that.

Let's Get Scared

Living longer, combined with working less, not investing at all, or investing too conservatively—which most investors do when given a choice as to how to invest their retirement dollars—might make for a carefree lifestyle today, but it could lead to a disaster later in life, particularly if you were to run out of money during your golden retirement years.

"The traditional path to the American Dream—working hard, earning, and saving—a path taken by our parents and their parents before them, no longer seems enough," says J. Carter Beese, Jr., former Commissioner of the U.S. Securities and Exchange Commission while addressing a 1993 Mutual Funds and Investment Management Conference. "The Dream—to give our children a better life, and in our golden years, live on the fruits of our hard work—seems at times, indeed, just a dream."

Unfortunately, even though more people today are receiving monthly income checks from Social Security than ever before, plus many receive retirement income from private pensions, the times are changing. Private companies are shifting the responsibility for how their employees' retirement accounts are managed. Responsibility for how those accounts get invested is being moved off the employers' shoulders and being placed squarely onto the shoulders of workers—people, who for the most part, have had no formal retirement planning education and readily admit that they know little or nothing about long-term money management.

As for Social Security, at the end of World War II there were 42 workers paying into Social Security for each person receiving benefits; today about 3 people contribute into that trust for every 1 person drawing money out of it. By the year 2030, it's estimated that 2 people will contribute for every 1 receiving benefits.

With the number of people contributing into Social Security decreasing and the number of people who will be calling upon that agency for their monthly checks increasing as our population ages, it doesn't take a rocket scientist to figure out that the future of Social Security—and what it asks of us and pays to us—is likely to change. How might it change? While it's impossible to see what the future will bring, here's a guesstimate of what some of those changes might be: everyone paying into Social Security might have to contribute more; those receiving benefits might receive less; and taxes on the income in benefits that Social Security checks provide might increase.

So, with corporate America shifting the onus of how money is invested for your retirement from their hands into yours, and with income from Social Security uncertain, the best way to prepare for having enough money to live on during your retirement years is to do the commonsense thing: create a plan for yourself, one that you are in charge of, know how to manage, and meets your own needs.

The Harsh Realities

In 1991, according to the U.S. Census Bureau, there were over 134 million full- and part-time workers in the United States. Fifty-one percent of them, or just over 69 million, were offered some kind of pension plan coverage by their employer. However only 40 percent, or 54 million workers, were participating in those plans.

If it surprises you that roughly half of the working people in the United States don't participate in their company's pension or retirement programs, be prepared for some more shocking news about how ill-prepared most Americans are regarding their retirement planning.

- According to The Fifth Annual Merrill Lynch Retirement Planning Survey, "Retirement Savings in America, 1993," at least half of employed households are not saving for retirement.
- Results of a study of 76 million U.S. households conducted jointly by the consulting firms of Arthur D. Little, Inc., and The WEFA Group and commissioned by Oppenheimer Management Corporation showed that nearly 8 out of every 10 U.S. households will have less than one-half of the annual income they will need to comfortably retire.

"Most Americans today did not live through the Great Depression, but at this rate, that's exactly what most people's retirements will be like," said Jon S. Fossell, Oppenheimer Management Corporation chairman and chief executive officer. "Relatively few Americans will be able to maintain their preretirement lifestyle once they stop working, and many will find themselves struggling simply to make ends meet."

Other findings from the Oppenheimer study were the following:

- 47 percent of all U.S. households are not covered by either a defined benefit or defined contribution plan.
- On average, married couples save 5.4 percent of their pretax income, single men save 3.1 percent, and single women, 1.5 percent.
- About 40 percent of workers who change jobs spend the lump-sum distributions they get instead of rolling them over into a new retirement plan.
- In the 1950s and 1960s, family income was rising faster than inflation, but in the 1980s and 1990s, family income after inflation has actually been declining.

And there's more:

- A survey conducted by the University of Michigan for Fidelity Investments concluded that two in five retirees will have no income except for that which Social Security provides. "Americans have developed a false sense of security about their retirement savings and think they don't have to curb their spending now to save more for the future," says Roger T. Servision, managing director at Fidelity Investments. "This survey clearly shows that Americans are not getting the job done and are facing an increased danger of out-living their retirement savings."

- About 80 percent of Americans underestimate how long they will live in retirement.

- Some retiring today on a $40,000 annual income will need $106,000 per year in income 20 years from now just to maintain their current standard of living if inflation averages 5 percent per year over those two decades.

CROWLEY'S FACTOIDS

Steve Crowley, a radio and television financial pro and author of *Money for Life,* offers these bottom-line factoids about retirement and retirement planning:

- Americans save less money annually than workers in any indus-trialized nation.

- By age 50, most Americans have accumulated less than $2500 for retirement. (That does *not* include monies in home equity or qual-ified retirement plans.)

- Fewer than 10 percent of Americans will retire financially secure at age 65. One-third of all will retire at or below the poverty level.

- Pension funds are currently seriously underfunded. A story in the *Palm Beach Post* on January 7, 1994, quoted Senator James M. Jeffords (R-VT) as saying: "The whole pension area is going to be the most serious problem facing the nation."

- The fastest-growing age group in the United States is those 85 years old and over. In 1990 there were 3 million people in that age group-ing; the Census Bureau says that by 2020 that number will swell to about 7 million.

Other Research

In a recent study commissioned by the American Association of Retired Persons (AARP) Investment Program and conducted by telephone, 829 adults 50 years of age and older were asked, "What could you have done to make yourself feel more financially prepared for the future?" Here are the three most frequent responses: 21 percent said they should have saved more money; 19 percent said they didn't know, and 13 percent responded with, "Start saving earlier."

The three most popular answers to the study question, "What is the biggest financial concern you face today?" were "Paying for health care," 18 percent; "Meeting day-to-day living expenses," 12 percent; and "Planning for retirement," 11 percent. Of those questioned, half had assets of $25,000 or less. (This number includes financial assets such as stocks or certificates of deposit and retirement plans but *not* the value of their own homes.) And in this group the biggest lifestyle concern was meeting day-to-day living expenses.

In another AARP study, preretirees (those between the ages of 45 to 59) were asked about their total retirement assets. Over two-thirds of respondents said that their assets, again excluding the value of their homes, amounted to less than $100,000; 32 percent said their assets were less than $20,000; and 14 percent said their assets were less than $5000.

Add to those numbers the fact that almost half, 46 percent, of those preretirees said they planned on retiring before age 65, and it's easy to see that many Americans are living in a dream state when it comes to being financially set for a 25-, 30-, or 40-year stint of nonworking retirement living.

These sources are all providing us with a loud retirement wake-up call, one that beckons the nearly retired to either save today or be prepared to downgrade their lifestyle tomorrow; the young to start saving for their future now; and the 76 million baby boomers heading toward those retirement doors to face the facts.

"Most baby boomers have grown up in a world where they assumed that their promised benefits and adequate retirement funds would be waiting for them at the end of their working years. Now, many of them are beginning to realize that the scene of an idyllic afternoon spent fishing, confident in knowing that an ample retirement check is in the mail, might be a thing of the past....And unfortunately, the sad truth is that for many baby boomers, it is," says J. Carter Beese, Jr., former Commissioner of the U.S. Securities and Exchange Commission.

Inflation: Believe It, It's Real

In 1947, the average income was $2854; the average new-home cost $6650; and the average car cost $1290. A loaf of bread cost 13 cents; a gallon of milk, 78 cents; and a gallon of gas, 15 cents.

Why don't things cost the same as they used to? Because of inflation. Inflation, the move upward in prices, happens as a result of supply and demand: too much money chasing too few goods or services.

It works like this: when you've got wads of money to spend and companies—like NIKE—are producing their goods (sneakers) as fast as they can yet the demand for those products (sports shoes) is greater than the supply, prices on those goods will go up. On the other hand, if vendors were selling NIKEs on every street corner in New York, Los Angeles, and Sioux Falls, and the supply of those soft-soled shoes far outweighed consumer demand, those pumped-up sneaker prices would fall.

I've always had a hard time believing the inflation projection numbers that I read about in the newspapers and hear on radio and television programs. You know, the ones that say a 4-year college education at a private school 20 years from now will run around a quarter of a million dollars. Or that you'll need at least a six- if not seven-figure nest egg to get you through your retirement years. Those numbers seem so hard to get a grip on.

If you have been as confounded about understanding the reality of inflation as I have, one way to see that, in fact, inflation really does exist is to look backward at your own life.

Remember back, 10, 15, 25, or 30 years in your own lifetime and compare the costs of living then with what they are now. If I look back to 1968, I was living in a charming rooming house on Boston's fashionable Beacon Street. There I shared a room in a brownstone with two other girlfriends. All three of us had traveled from our homes in Minnesota to start a new life in Boston. The cost for my share in our one room was $13 a week. At that time I was working as an engineering aide at Stone and Webster Engineering making $75 a week, bringing home 57 of those dollars. With that money I was able to pay my living expenses, have some fun bucks to spend, and even save some money. Right now that sounds so amazing to me. But it was true.

Today, $75 a week, or $3900 a year, isn't enough to live on. While that latter figure is not a bad monthly wage, it's a lousy annual one.

Not believing that inflation is a fact of life is one of the worst long-term financial planning mistakes anyone can make. Inflation is real. So the next time you'd rather not face up to that fact—or choose to only stockpile or spend all your money rather than to make a few investments with it—remember, there was a time not so long ago when 25 cents worth of gas in a Volkswagen's tank could take you quite a distance. And when 10,000 bucks a year was a big-time salary.

INFLATION RATES

Inflation affects our dollar's future buying power. A quick look at the accompanying chart shows the annual inflation rate for the years from 1980 to 1994. Although the inflation rate in the early 1990s isn't as high as it was in the early 1980s, it's still formidable.

Inflation Rate from 1980–1994

Year	Rate of inflation, %	Year	Rate of inflation, %
1980	12.7	1988	4.4
1981	8.9	1989	4.7
1982	3.8	1990	6.0
1983	3.8	1991	3.2
1984	3.9	1992	2.8
1985	3.8	1993	2.8
1986	1.0	1994	2.8
1987	4.4		

SOURCE: InvesTech Research.

Retirement: The Quiz

In March 1993 Fidelity Investments asked over 1000 people about retirement; the respondents were ages 25 and over, were not retired, and had annual incomes above $25,000. The results? Most flunked. The average score was a lousy 65 percent. That's equivalent to a failing grade by some standards, like those of a teacher I had in second grade, and a *D* by kinder and gentler others.

Following is the 10-question quiz those individuals were given. Why not take a few minutes to test yourself and see how retirement savvy you are?

1. Including Social Security and all other sources of income, in general, about what percentage of their income would you say most people need to maintain their lifestyle after retirement?
   a. Less than 20 percent
   b. 20 percent but less than 40 percent
   c. 40 percent but less than 60 percent
   d. 60 percent but less than 80 percent

2. In general, about what percentage of their total retirement income do you expect that most people will receive from Social Security and pension plans?

a. Less than 20 percent
b. 20 percent but less than 40 percent
c. 40 percent but less than 60 percent
d. 60 percent but less than 80 percent

3. Your monthly Social Security benefits may be reduced below what they may otherwise be if you retire before the age of 65.
   a. True
   b. False

4. Do you happen to know the earliest age an individual can collect Social Security benefits, assuming he or she is not handicapped or disabled?
   a. $59\frac{1}{2}$
   b. 62
   c. 65
   d. 67

5. Aside from those who are either handicapped or disabled, only those who have had a paying job are entitled to a Social Security check.
   a. True
   b. False

6. What phrase best describes what Medicare is?
   a. A health program for poor people
   b. A private health insurance program
   c. An HMO or health maintenance organization
   d. A federal health insurance program for the elderly

7. If a person switches jobs often during his or her working years, the pension benefits ultimately received might be reduced below what they might otherwise be.
   a. True
   b. False

8. If a person retires early, that person's monthly pension benefits from an employer ultimately received may be reduced below what they might otherwise be.
   a. True
   b. False

9. A person's pension plan benefits from an employer pension plan may be reduced if he or she also has an IRA account.
   a. True
   b. False

10. Anyone under the age of $70\frac{1}{2}$ with earned income is allowed to contribute to an IRA.

    a. True
    b. False

The answers are: 1. (*d*) 60 percent but less than 80 percent; 2. (*c*) 40 percent but less than 60 percent; 3. (*a*) True; 4. (*b*) 62; 5. (*b*) False; 6. (*d*) A federal health insurance program for the elderly; 7. (*a*) True; 8. (*a*) True; 9. (*b*) False; 10. (*a*) True.

Scoring:
Excellent: 9 out of 10 correct
Good: 8 out of 10 correct
Average: 7 out of 10 correct
Below Average: 6 out of 10 correct
Very Low: Less than 5 correct

2
Where Retirement Money Comes From

Ask a group of twenty-six-year-olds what they want to know about retirement, and the first answer you'll probably hear is a loud resounding, "Nothing!" Ask them a second time, and those twenty-somethings want to know exactly what everyone else wants to know about retirement, namely:

- How much money am I going to need to have to be able to retire?
- How, or where, am I going to get that money?

And that's about as straight as it gets!

How Much Money Am I Going to Need?

Knowing exactly how much money you're going to need to have socked away for retirement is a question that has a different answer for every single one of us. Which, I'd guess, is nine-tenths of the reason most of us don't save for our retirements—we don't know what the exact dollar goal is.

For someone living in Des Moines, $2000 a month might afford her or him a very comfortable retirement lifestyle income. For someone in Manhattan, that $2000 might just about cover one month's rent on a three-bedroom apartment, or the monthly maintenance on their condo. So the answer to the how-much-do-I-need question is, "It depends...."

It depends on things like where you live, how you like to live, and with whom you live. It also depends on a host of other variables, including the rate of inflation, how much money you've saved, what you did with the money you saved, and the kinds of results your invested dollars brought you. In other words, there's no one answer to that question that fits everybody.

Having said that, you can't make a long-term retirement plan without having a goal. So, to get a handle on what kind of money those retirement years can cost, look at what living life is costing you now, in terms of dollars and cents.

Here's a little six-step exercise to help you see first hand, based upon your individual lifestyle needs today, what the total cost of living for 20 or 30 years in retirement could amount to. Please keep in mind, the numbers tallied from this exercise do *not* take into account inflation or taxes. Nor are they any guarantee of what retirement will cost you. The purpose of the exercise is twofold:

1. To make you realize that retirement living isn't necessarily inexpensive. It costs money—probably more than you may have ever considered before.

2. To provide some basic numbers which you can use to begin your long-term retirement planning.

All that's needed to complete this next section is a pencil, a piece of paper, and the ability to know how to multiply and divide.

Start here:

1. Write down your age today on one line of a paper.

2. Choose the age at which you hope to retire. Then write that age down on the second line.

3. Decide how many years you will live after retirement (in other words, pick out an age at which you think you might die), and write that number on line 3 on the paper.

4. Based on your current lifestyle and living circumstances, write, on line 4 (*a*) the amount of money you spend each month and (*b*) the amount of money you spend each year. Use after-tax amounts of dollars here, as in take-home pay, and be realistic. For example, if you're currently bringing home $3000 a month after taxes, and realize that $4000 a month is what is necessary to cover your expenses, write in $4000 for (*a*) and $48,000 for (*b*). If $1200 a month suits you just fine, use $1200 for (*a*) and $14,400 for (*b*).

5. Take the annual dollar amount from line 4 and multiply it by the number of years you expect to live in retirement. Don't be stingy here. We are all living longer. So retiring at age 62 and living until age 68 isn't realistic anymore. (Unless of course you personally know otherwise.) So, if you plan to live 20 more years after you retire, and figure that living on $40,000 a year could be a good life, this calculation would be $40,000 × 20 = $800,000.

6. And—*voilà!* The figure you come up with from this exercise can serve as a starting point, providing you with an idea of what living for decades in retirement might cost. And in some cases, this number could even be a nest-egg goal—the amount you might want to have accumulated, or have access to, on the day you retire!

With that rough idea of what your own retirement might cost, the next question to answer is this one: How, or where, am I going to get that money?

Where Does Retirement Money Come From?

If you'd like to be wise beyond your years, don't count entirely on any one else—or any institution—to be your sole supporter during retirement. Companies and large corporations aren't the big-daddy providers they once were, especially when it comes to taking care of those they have employed via defined benefit retirement plans. Nor is Social Security the golden purse it once was. Which means, the one who is really left holding the Retirement Income Bag is *you!*

But before we look at how to develop a retirement plan that could yield hundreds of thousands of dollars, let's look at where today's retirees are currently getting their income.

The money that the retired—those aged 65 and older—have to spend typically comes from the following five different sources:

1. *Company retirement programs.* These are the employer-sponsored retirement plans. They come in two flavors: defined benefit plans and defined contribution plans. Defined benefit plans are pension plans created by an employer. In defined benefit plans, the company makes all the retirement investing decisions and invests on your behalf. Companies with defined benefit plans promise to pay their employees a set monthly retirement income the size of which is determined by a specific mathematical formula.

In defined contribution plans, it's either the employer, the employee, or both who directs where monies earmarked for retirement are to be invested. And it's the results of those investment choices—not some specific mathematical formula as in defined benefit plans—that determines the size of the retirement pie the employee receives. That's an important difference and means that because you have a hand in selecting how and where your retirement dollars are invested, it becomes essential for you to learn as much as possible about investing and how different investment products work. Quite conveniently, you will do so throughout the pages of this book.

2. *Personal savings, retirement plans, and inheritance.* Even though as a nation we're not the greatest savers, today's retirees say it's their own personal savings accounts—along with any personal investments that they've made, like IRAs and/or any retirement plans for the self-employed (like SEP-IRAs or Keoghs)—that end up being a great money source during retirement.

3. *Social Security.* The federal Social Security Administration provided over 26.4 million retired workers with monthly income checks in 1994. While that's a great "the check is in the mail" story, not everyone in the United States is covered by this pension program. For an employee to be eligible for Social Security pension benefits, there are some rules to follow. One is she or he has had to have paid FICA taxes, and have done so for a specified amount of time. If you've worked at a job in which FICA taxes were not taken out of your pay, don't expect to see a monthly Social Security check from your own working efforts. You could, however, receive one via the contributions your spouse has made.

4. *Personal investments.* Income from stocks, bonds, rental properties, or other kinds of investments made throughout a lifetime make up another source of a retiree's income.

5. *Continued employment.* There's no rule requiring someone to retire at age 65, and today more and more seniors are not. Many are either part- or full-time employees. The next time you're at a McDonald's or shopping at Wal-Mart take a look at the number of elderly Americans still in the workforce. Some seniors are working for the pleasure of it, others to supplement their incomes.

The amount of income a retiree receives from any of the above sources will vary depending on things like the kinds of jobs they held, the retirement plans they had access to and participated in, what investment choices they may or may not have made during their working careers (choosing not to invest is as much an investment decision as choosing to invest), how much money they were able to sock away in their savings accounts, and how much they are able to earn as employees in the "after retirement age" work arena.

A Social Security Administration study of the sources of retirees' incomes in 1993 divided those sources into six categories:

1. Social Security
2. Government pensions
3. Private pensions and annuities
4. Part-time or self-employment income
5. Assets (savings accounts or CDs, rental properties, stock dividends, bond interest, trust funds, and royalties)
6. Other (contributions from relatives, veteran's benefits, and income from public assistance programs)

The study showed that Social Security payments provide the lowest-income retirees with the highest percentage of their annual income (81 percent), whereas retirees with annual incomes of over $29,000 receive the lowest percentage of their annual incomes (20 percent) from that government program.

One very interesting finding concerned the role that income from assets played:

- For those with incomes of $11,000 a year, 6 percent came from the assets they had.
- For those with incomes of about $17,500, more than 11.5 percent came from their assets.
- For those with annual incomes of about $29,000, over 16 percent came from their assets.
- For those with incomes over $29,000, assets generated their primary source of income—representing 29 percent of their annual income.

Where Will *Your* Retirement Income Come From?

To get an idea of where your future retirement income is going to come from, look at where you stand today.

As we've pointed out, retirement income comes from sources including Social Security, pensions, retirement accounts, inheritances, or savings and investments. Unfortunately, not every one of us has access to all of those sources.

Here's a quick retirement income checklist to review. It's broken down into three broad groups based upon one's current work situation: working full-time, working part-time, and never worked. Use it as a guideline to see if you are taking advantage of the retirement investment opportunities currently available to you.

Working Full-Time

- Am I paying into Social Security via a FICA tax?
- Does my company offer a defined benefit or defined contribution retirement plan, and am I participating in it?
- Have I opened an IRA?
- Am I investing on my own, independent of Social Security or my company retirement plans?
- If I am self-employed, do I have a SEP-IRA or Keogh?
- What are the chances that I'll be inheriting any money?

Working Part-Time

- Am I paying into Social Security via a FICA tax?
- Does my company offer a defined benefit or defined contribution retirement plan and am I participating in it?
- If I am self-employed, am I contributing to a SEP-IRA or Keogh?
- Am I investing on my own, independent of Social Security or my company retirement plans?
- What are the chances that I'll be inheriting any money?

Never Worked

Social Security income is not applicable here, unless it's received from a spouse or because of special circumstances, and neither are employer-sponsored pension/retirement plans.

- What are the chances that I'll be inheriting any money?
- Am I contributing to an IRA?
- Am I investing—and saving—for retirement?

If you have never worked, knowing where the monies to live on will come from during retirement is particularly important. Nonworking spouses need to understand where and how the family income check(s) are spent and invested. Those without money concerns—either expecting an inheritance or a financial windfall—need to know how to invest their money so that it can provide them a lifelong income. All this means that no matter what your financial circumstances are or your employment situation is, we all need to address the question, Where will my retirement income come from?

3
Changing the Way You Look at Retirement

Becoming a Good Money Manager

Like it or not, we are all money managers. No matter if we are rich or poor, professional or blue-collar worker, under-the-table or salaried employee, male or female, adult or child, everyone who has had money cross their palm is a manager of the stuff.

Money, that medium of exchange used to pay for the goods and services we need and want, is something that's a part of each of our lives from before we are born until after we die. And while most of us aren't famous money managers, like Peter Lynch or Mario Gabelli (both have made their mark as well-known portfolio managers of successful mutual funds), like the pros we each make choices about what to do with the money that comes our way every time we receive our paychecks, get a money gift, or win a few bucks at the lottery or track.

Whether we use those bills and coins to keep the electricity flowing into our homes and apartments, for gas in our cars, to put food on our tables and clothes on our backs, or just to spend on the things we so desire, every time we take money in we then have to make a decision about what to do with it. That's a money management decision.

Think about that the next time you get your paycheck or someone gives you 20 dollars for your birthday. After that money is in your hot little hands—or often before, if you know it's coming—you make a decision about what to do with it.

When it comes to retirement, the trick to managing your money is to invest it for the long haul; the goal, of course, is to have put away enough money to be able to fund those retirement decades. There will be more discussion about money management and about how to develop short-, medium-, and long-term retirement investment goals in Parts 2 and 3 of the book. But for now the point is to realize the following:

- We are all money managers and are continually making choices about the money that comes our way. We can spend it all, or we can save some of it.

- Money management is a family affair. That is, every man, woman, and child needs to bone up on money management skills if they are to live financially productive lives—and have money to spend during their retirement. For more about teaching your children the right attitudes about money management, see Chapter 11.

Will You Have Enough Money for Your Retirement?

The key in calculating just how much money each of the different retirement income sources will provide us with (personal savings, pension and retirement accounts, Social Security) is, of course, the twenty-zillion-dollar question. It's also a question that people can only guess the answer to, unless they are right at or near the point of retirement and (1) have found out from Social Security what the size of their monthly checks will be, (2) have asked their employer what kind of income their retirement package will offer, and (3) have a good working knowledge of what their personal investments will yield.

Aside from that, the further people are away from their retirement years, the harder it is to calculate exactly what their income needs, or their money flow, will be.

There is, however, one way to ensure that money during your retirement won't be an issue that keeps you up at night. And that's to save, save, and save some more.

Becoming a Saver

"Saving for retirement is not a luxury, it's a necessity," says J. Carter Beese, Jr., former Commissioner of the U.S. Securities and Exchange Commission. And he's right.

Saving. That simple little six-letter word creates the floor from which most of us will build our asset base—unless, of course, we are lucky enough to inherit zillions or win a Publisher's Clearing House Sweepstakes. The odds of either, by the way, aren't good.

Saving money is one of the many lessons parents need to teach their children at as early an age as possible and remember to do themselves. It's a habit that we all need to participate in throughout our entire lifetimes.

Having money in the bank, tucked away in some secret place that only you know about, or invested, not only makes economic sense, it also makes most people feel good about themselves. I've yet to meet people who didn't stand a little taller, walk a little straighter, seem a little more sure of themselves when they had money in the bank and/or felt that their finances were in order. And having money in the bank, even if it's kept in low-yielding savings accounts, is much better than having no money stashed away at all.

But chances are, if you're like most Americans you're not saving enough money for your retirement. According to a Merrill Lynch survey titled Retirement Savings in America, in 1992 our net national savings rate—which means the sum of savings by government, businesses, and individuals—fell to 0.6 percent of gross domestic product (GDP), of course that's just over ½ of 1 percent. This percentage represents the lowest net national savings rate since World War II.

Another way to look at our personal savings rate is to see it as a percentage of our disposable income. (Disposable income is the amount of take-home money you receive after all state and local taxes, and the Social Security tax, have been deducted.)

On that score, we have nothing to brag about. As Fig. 3-1 shows, our personal savings rates as a percentage of our take-home pay averaged 6.7 percent during the 1960s; 7.7 percent during the 1970s; 6.5 percent during the 1980s; and a lowly 4.8 percent between 1990 and 1991. Clearly, we are a nation that prefers spending money rather than saving it. On the one hand, this fact may be considered good for the economy, but on the other, it is dreadful, particularly when it comes to funding one's retirement.

Most financial experts agree that people who save 10 percent of their salary, beginning with the first job they ever get, and then invest that money wisely, won't have a money problem 40 years later when it comes time to retire.

Even though most of us don't belong to this lucky group, remember: It's never too late to begin a savings program. If you're brand new to the notion of managing your money and would like to start a retire-

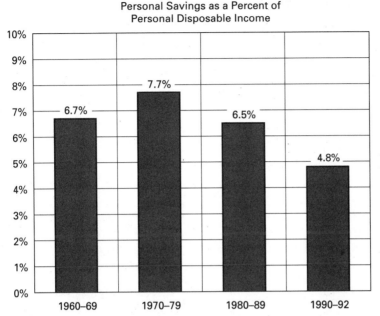

Figure 3-1. *How Much Do We Save?* A quick look at this chart shows that during the 1960s and the 1970s, Americans were better savers then than they were in the 1980s and are in the 1990s. [*Source: Securities Industry Association (SIA)*]

ment savings plan, it's important to realize that every cent that comes your way, plain and simple, provides an opportunity for *you* to make a choice as to how it gets used.

The bottom line is that it's you who is in charge of your money and not the other way around. Even for people living from paycheck to paycheck, choosing how money gets spent winds up to be a matter of priorities.

Prioritizing money is like pigeon-holing it. And it can be a whole lot easier to accomplish than one might think—once you have accepted responsibility for it.

Throwing spare change from your pockets or the bottom of your handbag into a dish or jar and, when that's full, putting that change into a savings account is a no-brainer way to save. So is transferring payments: once you've paid off your car or that college loan, keep those money payments going. Except this time use the monies to fund your retirement account.

Five Ways to Save Money

Saving money for retirement can be habit-forming.

"There's momentum in saving," says Sharon Barnes, a mother of three in Denver. "Once I began saving, watching that money grow made me want to save more. It becomes almost a game—to see how much I can make that money grow to."

If you are stumped about how to begin saving for your retirement, here are five good commonsense starter ideas:

1. *Pay yourself first.* Have your bank automatically transfer a specific amount of money each month from your checking account into a savings account—or an investment account, mutual fund account, or retirement plan. Do this with as little or as much money as you can afford, making sure the amount meets the minimum investment requirements of your investment choices. Then increase the contribution annually, if possible. Paying yourself for the work you do is not only financially rewarding, it's a self-image booster as well and doesn't cost much. Many mutual fund accounts have minimum investment requirements of $25 or $50. Savings accounts also don't require large outlays of money.

2. *Can most of the credit cards.* It's difficult to live in today's world without having at least one full-service credit card to your name. But having a wadful of these cards is unnecessary, expensive, and may be costly to your long-term financial well-being. Not only are the interest rate fees that credit card companies charge high, but if you only pay the minimum amount due on that debt each month, it takes years to pay off the balances.

Dee Lee, a financial educator in Harvard, Massachusetts, says that if someone has a $2000 balance on a credit card that's charging 18 percent a year for its use and that person is only making the minimum monthly payments on that card, it will take 33 years to pay that debt off in full. Yikes!

3. *Understand diversification.* Spread your retirement monies around. Don't keep all of it in the bank or all in mutual funds. But do have some money in conservative places like a savings account, bank CDs, or Treasury securities as well as some in more aggressive investments like stocks and/or stock and bond funds.

4. *Take advantage of all the retirement programs available to you.* For instance, open an IRA. Or if you are employed, participate in your company's 401(k) retirement plan or any of the qualified retirement plans it offers. If you are self-employed, open a Keogh or SEP-IRA for yourself. In other words, don't overlook any retirement-plan opportunities.

5. *Watch the clock.* Set up realistic financial time frames in which to allow your money to work. Decide for yourself what short, medium, and long term mean. Then see whether your personal definitions of time match up with both those of the products you're investing in and your personal financial goals.

Once you and the product(s) you've selected are on the same wavelength as far as short-, medium-, and long-term goals are concerned, evaluate the performance of those investment choices accordingly. For instance, retirement money that's earmarked for long-term growth ought to be invested in securities that have shown strong long-term results. Money needed in the short term, as in six months to a year, needs to be conservatively managed.

GETTING OUT FROM UNDER

If you're caught in a money crunch, with no seemingly disposable cash at hand, here's a tip from financial author and planner Jonathan Pond: To come up with a long-term plan, write down the biggest money problems you have right now and then make a decision to get over them.

"Open a savings account and deposit money into it, rain or shine," says Pond. "Saving money is the first step in building financial security."

START NOW

The sooner you start saving, the faster your money grows. As the following chart shows, if you invest $2000 annually for 8 years beginning at age 25, stop at age 32, and let your savings compound annually at an 8 percent rate, your money will grow to $269,661 by age 64. Waiting 10 years to begin saving would mean you must invest $44,000 . more of your own money over a *30-year* time frame to have even a comparable retirement savings figure at age 64—and you would still come up almost $25,000 short.

Age	Deposit	Year-end value	Deposit	Year-end value
25	$2,000	$2,160	$-0-	—
26	$2,000	4,493	-0-	—
27	$2,000	7,012	-0-	—
28	$2,000	9,733	-0-	—
29	$2,000	12,672	-0-	—
30	$2,000	15,846	-0-	—
31	$2,000	19,273	-0-	—
32	$2,000	22,975	-0-	—
33	-0-	24,813	-0-	—
34	-0-	26,798	-0-	—
35	-0-	28,942	2,000	$2,160
36	-0-	31,257	2,000	4,493
37	-0-	33,758	2,000	7,012
38	-0-	36,459	2,000	9,733
39	-0-	39,375	2,000	12,672
40	-0-	42,525	2,000	15,846
41	-0-	45,927	2,000	19,273
42	-0-	49,602	2,000	22,975
43	-0-	53,570	2,000	26,973
44	-0-	57,855	2,000	31,291
45	-0-	62,484	2,000	35,954
46	-0-	67,482	2,000	40,991
47	-0-	72,881	2,000	46,430
48	-0-	78,711	2,000	52,304
49	-0-	85,008	2,000	58,649
50	-0-	91,809	2,000	65,500
51	-0-	99,154	2,000	72,900
52	-0-	107,086	2,000	80,893
53	-0-	115,653	2,000	89,524
54	-0-	124,905	2,000	98,846
55	-0-	143,898	2,000	108,914
56	-0-	145,689	2,000	119,787
57	-0-	157,345	2,000	131,530
58	-0-	169,932	2,000	144,212
59	-0-	183,527	2,000	157,909
60	-0-	198,209	2,000	172,702
61	-0-	214,065	2,000	188,678
62	-0-	231,191	2,000	205,932
63	-0-	249,686	2,000	224,566
64	-0-	269,661	2,000	244,692
TOTAL DEPOSIT	$16,000		$60,000	

SOURCE: Transamerica Funds.

Investing $2000 for eight years between the ages of 33 and 40
would yield $145,689. (Please note: No taxes have been taken out in

these examples, all interest is reinvested, and money is left to grow and compound.)

	$2000 annual @ 8%	
Age	Contribution	Value
25	0	0
26	0	0
27	0	0
28	0	0
29	0	0
30	0	0
31	0	0
32	0	0
33	2,000	2,160
34	2,000	4,493
35	2,000	7,012
36	2,000	9,733
37	2,000	12,672
38	2,000	15,846
39	2,000	19,273
40	2,000	22,975
41	0	24,813
42	0	26,798
43	0	28,942
44	0	31,257
45	0	33,758
46	0	36,459
47	0	39,375
48	0	42,525
49	0	45,927
50	0	49,602
51	0	53,570
52	0	57,855
53	0	62,484
54	0	67,482
55	0	72,881
56	0	78,711
57	0	85,008
58	0	91,809
59	0	99,154
60	0	107,086
61	0	115,653
62	0	124,905
63	0	134,898
64	0	145,689

SOURCE: Transamerica Funds.

The moral to this story is one you might recall from your childhood: The early bird gets the worm.

The High Cost of Retirement Living

One of the big could-not-be-trues floating around is that life becomes much cheaper in old age. For some that might be so, but for many others, retirement years' out-of-pocket costs can tally as much if not more than their nonretirement years did. This is true especially for those who are always on the go, or for those who need 24-hour health care and have been caught ill-prepared for the high cost of medical care.

Financial experts estimate that people will need in the neighborhood of 60 to 80 percent of their current working income to be able to maintain their current lifestyle after retirement. Keep in mind that those "60 to 80 percent" figures are only guidelines designed to provide us with some nest-egg dollar goals from which to make our long-term investment plans.

Jerry Alcorn is a 75-year-old retiree spending his senior years in Arizona. When he retired from his building inspector career at age 65, Alcorn was bringing home, after taxes, about $2000 a month. Today his monthly living expenses are still running around $2000 a month.

Where does he get that $2000? About $1300 of it each month comes from Social Security and his pension benefits. The rest, about $700, comes from incomes from rental property that he owns.

Alcorn said that even though some costs of living life in retirement are cheaper (he doesn't have a mortgage on his home, for instance, nor does his wardrobe need to be updated regularly), other living expenses still keep rising.

"The big increases I feel are in health care costs and food," he says. "Plus things like taxes on my property and my income along with car and property insurance are always going up. Never mind what it costs to play a round of golf these days."

His story isn't an unusual one. A reduced cost of living during your retirement years isn't a guarantee. So don't assume that you'll get by on the cheap in those golden years. Those years can number in the dozens and cost in the plenties.

Who Said You Have to Retire at Age 65?

Looking into the future and the coming new century, chances are many of us will be working beyond age 65 and perhaps well into our seventies or even eighties. Gerontology working could, in fact, turn out to be the rage.

I asked Phyllis Diller, the comedian, when she was planning to retire.

"For me, retirement and death will be synonymous! Besides, I don't have to retire because I'm not working for a company, I'm working for me. And every day I get better at my job. So why would I ever fire someone who is finally getting enough experience to be hot stuff?"

Working into the seventh and eighth decades of our lives might not be a choice for all of us, as it is for Ms. Diller, but a necessity. Why? Again, because we are living longer and not preparing financially for our longer lifespan.

"Around the turn of the century [1900] people started working earlier, they worked longer, retired later, and consequently the accumulation stage of their wealth span was longer," says Neal Cutler, director of the Boettner Institute of Financial Gerontology at the University of Pennsylvania. "And because life expectancy was shorter, the expenditure stage was also shorter.

"By 1990, people entered the labor force later and retired earlier, so the accumulation stage is now shorter. At the same time, however, because we live longer the expenditure stage is also longer....This means that we have to accumulate more resources in a shorter time. And the resources must last for a longer time...."*

So one way of beating the I-don't-have-enough-money-to-retire problem is to continue working, full- or part-time, like the stars do.

*The Financial Monitor Newsletter, April–May 1994, p. 1.

PART 2
Retirement Plans

4
What You Need to Know

Understanding the products and the jargon in the world of retirement isn't easy. If you're in the woods regarding what kinds of retirement plans and investment options are available to you, don't worry, you're not alone.

Throughout this chapter and the next, you'll learn about the different kinds of retirement programs and come to grips with the differences between Keoghs, CODAs, ESOPs, and 401(k)s. It may help you to keep in mind that all company-sponsored retirement plans are variations of what our grandparents called "pension plans."

What Is a Pension Anyway?

According to *Webster's Dictionary*, the word *pension* comes from the Latin word *pendere* and means "to pay." One of the big carrots used by large companies and corporations to attract employees has, historically, been the benefits packages offered. Such benefits packages included, among other things, a good pension.

Pension plans got their first start in the United States well over 350 years ago. Throughout the centuries they have grown in both number of plans and number of participants. Today, according to *The World Almanac and Book of Facts 1994*, two-thirds of the work force is covered by some type of pension. (As pointed out earlier, not all employees take advantage of the pension plans offered them.)

One of the first, if not the first, pension plans was the Plymouth Colony settlers' military retirement program created in 1636. More than one hundred years later, in 1759, a plan created for the benefit of widows and children of Presbyterian ministers came along. And, according to the Employee Benefit Research Institute (EBRI), a nonprofit organization that oversees employee benefits, the first corporate pension plan appeared on the scene in 1875. It was established by American Express.

In the 100 years between 1875 and 1975, more than 400 different pension plans were created. Industries providing pension plans to their employees during that time frame were generally the banking, railroad, and public utility ones. By the early 1990s there were more than 850,000 different pension plans around that covered more than 44 million workers. These plans can be found throughout companies in all kinds of industries, from the largest corporations to the smallest private businesses.

That's the good news. The bad news is (1) not all pension benefits packages are created equally, (2) many employees do not understand the retirement plans offered to them, and (3) the number of employees not participating in employer-sponsored plans is staggering. You learned in Chapter 2 that only 40 percent of employees are participating in their company-sponsored retirement programs. That means that 60 percent aren't participating. And if 60 percent of employees aren't saving for their retirement through an employer-sponsored retirement plan, then the majority of working Americans are not taking advantage of this financial opportunity. This opportunity could provide some additional money to spend during retirement and could make a big difference in the kind of lifestyle, as well as in the quality of life, enjoyed during their upcoming retirement decades.

Learning the Language

> I've never looked at the 401(k) plan my company's got because I think I won't make enough money to be able to participate in it.
> —A MEAT CUTTER FROM SOUTHERN CALIFORNIA

Although you won't learn the specifics of the hundreds of thousands of benefits plans floating around today by reading this book, you will definitely learn enough about the basics from which these plans are created. And you'll learn enough not to be in the same boat as the California worker quoted above—who is missing a prime retirement investment opportunity.

But before we get into the vocabulary, keep in mind the following important points.

1. To participate knowledgeably in any long-term retirement plan, you need to be well informed about what kinds of retirement plans are

available and also about the different investment options, or choices, that are offered within those plans.

2. How much money you make has nothing to do with whether or not you are allowed to participate in your company's retirement benefits package, if they provide one. There may be caps placed on the total amount you may add annually to your company retirement plan but don't let those maximum amounts keep you from contributing whatever is affordable.

3. If your employer isn't offering a retirement plan, don't worry. You can create one for yourself. Conventional ways to plan for your retirement include starting a savings plan, opening an individual retirement account, investing in a tax-deferred annuity, and/or creating your own investment portfolio of stocks, bonds, and/or mutual funds, each chosen specifically with the long-term investment objective of providing you and your loved ones with the income you'll need during your retirement years.

4. And even if you are participating in your employer's retirement program, or in any self-employed retirement plan, like a Keogh or a SEP-IRA, you can also open an IRA each and every year for yourself. While there are rules regarding how much, if any, of that IRA contribution may be deducted from your taxes each year, *any* money invested in an IRA grows tax-deferred until it is withdrawn.

The Big Picture

Two of the biggest problems facing anyone wanting to participate in retirement plans—like those offered via your employer or the ones that you can set up for yourself—are knowing (1) what kinds of retirement plans are available and (2) what different kinds of investment options, or choices, you can make within those plans. Point 1 is addressed in the rest of this chapter, which discusses the generic differences between types of plans (qualified versus nonqualified plans and defined benefit versus defined contribution plans), and Chapter 5, which gives details about specific plans. The different kinds of investment products are covered in Part 3.

Qualified and Nonqualified Plans

A *qualified plan* is one in which an employer sets up and contributes to his employees' retirement plans. For doing so, that employer receives some tax breaks for his company from Uncle Sam. To be eligible for these tax breaks, qualified plans must satisfy the rules of the Internal

Revenue Code (IRC) and the Employee Retirement Income Security Act of 1974 (ERISA). ERISA was signed into law by President Gerald Ford on Labor Day in 1974. Some of the things the Act does is "set specific standards for eligibility, coverage participation, vesting, benefit accrual, and funding of retirement plans." Thus ERISA is the legislation governing the actions of the qualified-plan retirement world. That means any company offering an employer-sponsored retirement program in which the company receives tax incentives for providing pension plans to their employees must follow the rules set out in this Act.

A plan labeled *nonqualified* is one that doesn't qualify the company that sponsors it for tax deductions. Keep in mind that the growth of money invested in either a qualified or nonqualified plan compounds tax-deferred.

Defined Benefit and Defined Contribution Plans

Retirement benefits packages come in two types: defined contribution plans or defined benefits plans. Both defined benefits plans and defined contribution plans are regulated by the IRC and ERISA through the Internal Revenue Service and the Department of Labor. Here's what these terms mean.

Defined Benefit Plans. *Defined benefit plans* include any pension program that your company makes available to you in which the company does all the funding and makes all the choices as to where retirement monies are invested. Defined benefit plans are the granddaddies of the pension world. They represent the kinds of pension programs in which the employer is truly the Big Boss when it comes to deciding how or where pension monies are invested. Determining how much of those pension monies you'll receive at retirement time is based upon a specific mathematical formula that depends on your compensation and years of service to your employer.

If you work for a company that provides its employees with a pension based upon a defined benefit plan, when it comes time to receive your cut of this retirement pie, the exact amount of your monthly income—or stipend—will be calculated and then divvied out according to that prescribed formula.

The three most common formulas used in calculating how much employees will receive at retirement from their defined benefits plans are flat-benefit formulas, career-average formulas, and final-pay formulas. Each is figured in its own unique way, again depending upon one's years of service to a company as well as on that person's pay level.

According to the U.S. Department of Labor, in 1993, 56 percent of full-time employees of medium-sized and large companies were covered by defined benefit plans. If the company you work for offers a defined benefit plan, you won't be left in the dark regarding how much money you'll receive at retirement. Nor will you have had to manage your retirement assets—that job is the employer's.

There are some drawbacks to defined benefit plans. The primary one is to be eligible to receive any retirement benefits an employee has to be *vested,* that is, to have worked for that company a certain number of years.

Vesting. Vesting has to do with your right to receive retirement benefits from your employer. The rules of vesting differ from company to company and center around the length of time you've worked for an employer.

There are two different vesting timetables employers use. One is called *cliff* vesting. It means, for example, that after five years of participating in an employer's retirement plan one would be fully, or 100 percent, vested in that pension program. The other is *gradual* vesting. Vesting here happens in stages, for example: After 3 years of participation in a retirement plan one becomes 20 percent vested in it; after 4 years, 40 percent vested; and so on until at the end of the seventh year, one would be fully vested in the company's retirement program.

If you work for an employer offering a defined contribution retirement plan, like a 401(k), any and all monies you personally have invested into that account will move with you when you change jobs. But the money, if any, your employer has added will move only if your years of service to that employer meet that company's vesting schedule.

Defined Contribution Plans. *Defined contribution plans* are pension plans in which the employer, the employee, or both may make contributions into your retirement account. These plans include 401(k) and 403(b) plans, SEP-IRAs, profit-sharing plans, employee stock ownership plans (ESOPs), money-purchase plans, and thrift and savings plans.

Numbers from the U.S. Department of Labor show that, in 1993, 49 percent of full-time employees in medium-sized and large companies participated in one or more defined contribution plans.

When it comes time to retire, the size of your defined contribution nest egg will depend on things such as:

- How much—and for how long—the employer and/or you, the employee, have contributed to the plan.

- How well the pension monies were invested.
- What the market conditions were like during that investment time period.

As we all know, how any investment performs is a lot like how our gardens grow. Both are subject to conditions and cycles outside of our control; both have to be tended and watched; and both provide us with yields that more often than not can be surprising.

Defined contribution plans are the "in" retirement plan these days. According to *Worth* magazine (December/January 1994) there are currently 16 million employees who contribute some $36 billion a year to 185,000 different defined contribution plans. In fact, chances are if your company isn't offering a defined contribution plan to its employees today, it probably will be tomorrow.

ROLLOVERS

Taking money out of one qualified tax-sheltered retirement account and moving it into another is called a *rollover*. Today the most efficient way to roll over monies is through a "trustee-to-trustee" rollover and, unlike the old days when those transferring money from one account into another actually got their hands on that money, trustee-to-trustee rollovers don't allow that. They are an efficient, and currently the only, way of rolling money over without incurring penalties.

Money gets rolled over from one tax-deferred retirement account into another when people leave their jobs or decide to make some changes as to where their retirement dollars are being invested.

To roll over any of your retirement plan dollars, you've got to do some preplanning and paperwork. Check into the paperwork that trustee-to-trustee rollovers require before leaving your job or selecting another retirement investment vehicle.

Remember, rollovers between IRAs can only happen once every 12 months *and* must be completed within 60 days from receipt of the distribution. That's the law.

Some of the advantages to defined contribution plans are:

1. Employees can reap handsome financial rewards depending upon how well the money in these accounts is managed.

2. As time goes on, the number of choices as to where and how retirement monies in defined contribution plans can be invested is likely

to broaden. Plus, you can change your mind about where your money is invested: generally, at least once a year you'll have an opportunity to redirect how all, or a portion of, those retirement monies are being invested.

3. Typically, employees receive a lump-sum payout from defined contribution plans when they leave their job. Consequently, they are faced with a decision to make: (a) take that money, pay the penalties and taxes on it, and spend it or (b) avoid paying the penalties and defer paying the taxes on the money by rolling it over into an IRA account. Although most people choose (a), the wiser retirement planning move is to choose (b).

4. The rules for vesting in defined contribution plans may be more liberal than the ones of defined benefit programs. In defined contribution plans, all employee contributions are vested immediately.

There are also some drawbacks:

1. The investment performance of defined contribution plans depends upon things like the product choices you or your boss makes, market conditions, and how long you've been a part of this retirement plan. So knowing exactly how much money you'll receive from a defined contribution plan can be difficult to calculate accurately ahead of time.

2. In most cases employees know little about making long-term investment choices. That means, the better educated you are about investments, the better your chances are of making wise retirement planning choices. (See the following inset.)

EMPLOYEE-DIRECTED DEFINED CONTRIBUTION PLANS

There's a trend going on. And it's not one in fashions, lifestyles, or vacation destinations—although how well you manage your retirement dollars could easily impact the style in which you'll live through the last quarter of your life.

The trend involves you and your employer-sponsored defined contribution retirement plan and focuses on responsibility.

Today, more and more employers are offering their workers defined contribution kinds of retirement packages in which it's the employee and not the employer who directs where one's retirement monies are to be invested. The responsibility for where one's retirement dollars get invested is being shifted off of the shoulders of the boss and placed squarely upon those of the employees.

What this means to employees is that if they really don't know anything about long-term investing, they've got to learn as soon as possible.

If you're an employee of a company offering a defined contribution retirement plan, like a 401(k), and just the idea of managing your own retirement monies makes you shudder, the quickest way to learn about the long-term rewards of investing for your retirement is to ask questions.

To get into the inquiring mind mode, here's a list of 15 questions that you may want to ask your employer, or employee benefits representative, about the employer-sponsored defined contribution retirement plan.

1. What is the exact name of the employer-sponsored retirement plan that's offered?

2. Would you please define what that plan is and what it means for me?

3. Are there choices as to where and how I can invest my money in this retirement plan?

4. If so, what are those choices? And is there information or prospectuses for me to read explaining the different investment choices?

5. How much money, or what percentage of my salary, may I invest into the program each year? And, how do I do that?

6. Will you, my employer, be making any matching contributions to this plan?

7. If so, what will you contribute each year, and what are the conditions of your contributions?

8. May I change my mind and redirect where my money gets invested once I begin participating?

9. If so, how often can I do that? Are there going to be any costs or fees passed on to me for making a change in my choice of investments?

10. Will there be any ongoing or annual fees passed on to me in these plans?

11. If so, how much are they, and how will those fees affect my investment returns?

12. What are the performance track records of the investments available to me in the defined contribution plan that you're offering? Also, what sources can I use to compare those performance numbers with to see which investments are worth putting my money into?

13. Once I begin contributing to this retirement plan, can I stop making contributions now and then? Or must I continue to do so year in and year out?

14. If, or when, I leave this company, what procedures must I follow to take my defined contribution retirement monies with me? Can I elect to leave them here?

15. Whom do I come to with any investing questions relating to my employer-sponsored retirement plans?

Remember *before* visiting your firm's employee benefits representative to jot down the questions that you want to ask, and be sure to bring along a pencil and paper to take notes.

5
A Closer Look at the Options

Employee Stock Ownership Plans (ESOPs)

Louis O. Kelso is the man credited with creating the idea of ESOPs. Because any holder of stock is an owner of the corporation that stock represents, Kelso thought employees receiving shares of their company's stock, or an indirect interest in it, would not only be inspired to be more productive, but would be provided with a means of sharing in the capital success of their company. Good thinking, wouldn't you say?

According to the National Center for Employee Ownership, in 1979 there were 1601 ESOP programs around. At that time, about a quarter of a million employees participated in those programs. As of 1989, the number of plans had swelled to 10,237 with over 11.5 million employees enjoying the benefits of stock ownership via ESOP programs.

Just as you might imagine, ESOPs are retirement plans which invest primarily in the stock of the employer. The employees participating in ESOPs don't have to spend their own money to buy the shares of the stock; their employers purchase it for them through plan contributions. And when it comes time to retire, the employees may either take their pension proceeds in stock certificates or in a cash amount equal to the value of the stock.

Because it's the employer who is contributing the stock to their employees' retirement plans, the corporation offering this kind of plan gets some nifty tax benefits.

Who Can Participate? Anyone working for a corporation offering this kind of retirement plan can participate.

Some Pluses

1. Anyone participating in a company's ESOP program has certain voting privileges.
2. ESOPs give employees the opportunity to share in the growth of their company if that stock increases in value.
3. Participants are also entitled to receive any dividends that the company pays its shareholders.

Some Minuses

1. Performance varies. The value of a stock changes over time, fluctuating up and down as the markets change. While the long-term history of the stock market has been a positive one, how much money your company's stock will provide to you at retirement will depend upon the number of shares owned and the price of the company's stock once you begin selling off the shares.
2. ESOPs are not always well-diversified investments. Investing in only one stock can be very risky. If it performs well, that's great. But if the company has problems or goes broke, your retirement income might not be what you'd hoped for. Look at IBM, for example. In September of 1987, the per-share price of IBM stock was around $160. At year-end 1992, it was trading in the $40 range. That one instance shows how important diversifying your retirement assets is. (Some ESOP programs do allow for retirement monies to be diversified. Ask your employer about the specifics.)

Who Regulates? The Internal Revenue Code (IRC) and the Employee Retirement Income Security Act (ERISA), through the Internal Revenue Service and the Department of Labor, regulate ESOP plans.

Who Makes the Investment Selections? The company offers the investments. If the company you're working for is flying high and its stock price is soaring, when it comes time to tally up the value of your shares and retire, you might be sitting pretty. On the other hand, stock prices don't always increase in value. They usually fluctuate up and down in value.

If you're a part of an ESOP plan and currently investing into only your company's stock, make sure to have some retirement monies invested elsewhere. Keeping all your retirement nest egg in one basket can be costly.

To learn more about your firm's ESOP program, ask your boss to direct you to the person who handles employee benefits at your company.

401(k)s

It's hard to pick up a financial magazine—like *Money, Worth,* or *Forbes*—or peruse the business section of your local newspaper without reading something about 401(k)s. 401(k) plans are defined contribution payroll-deduction plans in which monies are taken directly from a worker's salary and invested in a tax-deferred retirement plan.

401(k)s are currently the darling of the investment arena: financial planners and advisors, accountants, mutual funds, and company benefits coordinators are spreading the word about these pension plans, which are named after the section of the Internal Revenue Code (IRC) they represent.

In most 401(k) plans, you, the employee, decide to have money taken out of your wages, and you instruct your plan coordinator to put it directly into the investment plan you have selected. One plus to 401(k)s is that you don't have to pay taxes on the portion of your income that's contributed to the plan until retirement or until money from that account is withdrawn.

The big push by financial institutions and experts encouraging people to participate in their company's 401(k) plans is based upon a couple of things. First, retirement planning is something we all have to learn about, and a *must do* for every employee today. And second, these plans can benefit both employers and employees. Employers can get some tax breaks provided they are contributing to their employees' 401(k) accounts, and also they aren't responsible for paying retirement benefits as they would be in defined benefits plans. For employees, the benefits include the ability to pick and choose their own investment products and immediate vesting for the money they contribute to their 401(k).

Employers generally like payroll-deduction 401(k)s because they no longer have to take full responsibility for where their employees' retirement dollars get invested. Plus, such a retirement benefit plan isn't as costly to the company as, say, a defined benefit plan might be. Recent studies show that a typical pension plan costs a company 4 to 6 percent of its payroll while the costs for offering 401(k) plans are easily half that amount: 1.5 to 2 percent.*

Employees generally like 401(k)s—sometimes called a "company savings plan"—for a number of reasons:

1. There are a variety of places into which 401(k) money can be invested, including

- Guaranteed investment contracts (GICs), which are insurance products that invest in fixed-income securities
- Mutual funds, which are diversified and professionally managed portfolios of stocks, bonds, and money-market instruments offering a wide variety of choices as to where and how your money gets invested, along with opportunities to invest that money conservatively, moderately, or aggressively
- Individual stocks
- Individual corporate bonds

2. Every cent that employees contribute to their own 401(k) gets taken out of their paycheck. That means you don't have to pay income taxes on those contributions in the year that money is deducted. Taxes are postponed until you withdraw the money.

That's the good news. The bad news is that even though your 401(k) contributions are taken right off the top of your salary, and invested on your behalf into a retirement plan in which the monies can compound and grow tax-deferred, you'll have less money to bring home every pay period. Plus, the Social Security tax still has to be paid on the *full* amount of your wages, including the amount invested into the 401(k).

3. There is "free money" floating around for many participants of 401(k) plans. According to a study conducted by Hewitt Associates, 84 percent of companies offering these kinds of retirement plans "match" their employees contributions. To match contributions means that if you're adding money to your retirement plan, the company you work for is doing so also. For example, let's say for every $1 you put into your 401(k) your company might match it with a 25- or 50-cent contribution. Those matching contributions can make a big difference in the size of your retirement nest egg. So make sure to take advantage of this free-money opportunity. One final thought: Even if your employer doesn't offer a matching contribution plan, don't let that stop you from contributing all you can to a 401(k).

*Jeff Blyskoll, "How Good Is Your Company's 401(k) Plan?" *Worth,* December–January 1994.

The following inset shows how fast money in a 401(k) plan can grow when that money is left to compound and grow tax-deferred.

WHY PARTICIPATE?

There is no denying that money left to grow and compound tax-deferred—that is, allowed to grow without taxes being taken from it—grows faster and quicker than accumulated money that has taxes taken from it annually.

To show how great a tax-deferred edge can be over time, the following chart compares the returns on a $200 a month ($2400 a year) investment for 30 years, at an annual investment return of 8 percent, for (1) a taxable savings plan and (2) a tax-deferred investment vehicle like a 401(k). (This example assumes that the investor is in the 28 percent tax bracket.) The 30-year return for the taxable plan is $138,847, compared with a whopping $300,058 for the tax-deferred plan.

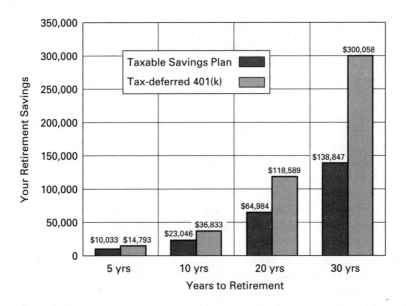

SOURCE: Scudder, Stevens and Clark, Inc.

---

4. Another plus for the 401(k) is vesting: You are always 100 percent vested for all of the tax-deferred contributions, and their earnings, that you make into your 401(k). So, any monies personally invested along

with monies accrued from your investment goes with you should you leave that company or change jobs.

Therefore, it doesn't matter if you've been a part of your company's 401(k) program for 1 month or for 10 years, your contribution moves with you.

However, money that the company contributes might not. There are vesting rules that apply to company contributions to 401(k)s. Consequently, whatever contributions an employer makes to your account may or may not travel with you. For the intricacies on that issue check with your employer's benefits package coordinator.

5. Finally, participating in a 401(k) plan may save some money on your taxes. Depending upon how much money was contributed, your tax bracket could be lowered come April 15. But don't count on that break until you've put the pencil to it and precisely calculated your taxes.

Note: Of the more than 24 million employees currently eligible to participate in 401(k)s, about 13 million do. The typical company contributes 33 cents for every dollar contribution an employee makes. The average employee contributes $2100 per year and the company $700.

Who Can Participate? Anyone who works for a for-profit company that's offering this kind of retirement program can participate in it.

Some Pluses

1. Choice: Although the 401(k) investment choices will differ from company to company, employees will have a say as to where and how conservatively or aggressively their retirement dollars are invested.

2. There's "free money" available to you when your company matches any portion of your 401(k) contributions.

3. Beginning in January 1994, the U.S. Labor Department put into action some rules that may help 401(k) participants. Basically the rules require that any company sponsoring these programs, that wants to minimize its responsibility for investment decisions, has to provide its employees with a minimum of three investment choices—like a stock fund, bond fund, and a money-market mutual fund—along with some risk and reward profiles so that the employees can have a sense of what the ups and downs of their investment choices could be.

4. Any money you put into a 401(k) is always yours. This means that your personal 401(k) contributions are 100 percent vested as soon as the first penny is added to the plan.

Some Minuses

1. Getting at your 401(k) money before you retire, or reach age 59½, typically means paying some IRS penalties—except when you can prove a hardship exists. As in other retirement plans, like IRAs and Keoghs, these retirement monies aren't available to you penalty-free until you are at least age 59½. Taking money out before then comes with a 10 percent penalty. Penalties also apply when waiting too long to withdraw the money or when taking too much out in any given year.

2. Not all 401(k) plans are created equally. The company you work for creates the plan it wants to offer. Which means the investment choices allowed in 401(k) plans will differ from company to company. Consequently, some plans are better than others.

3. Transferring accumulated savings into a different kind of retirement program outside of the one offered by your employer—as teachers can with 403(b) plans—can't happen with 401(k)s. The only time the money becomes yours to transfer into another retirement account—outside of the ones offered by your employer—is when you leave your job. Your options are explained in the upcoming inset.

4. There are limits to the amount you can contribute to a 401(k) each year. In the 1995 tax year, the maximum amount you can contribute to your tax-deferred 401(k) is $9240 or 20 percent of your salary, whichever is less.

WHEN YOU CHANGE JOBS

When changing employers, whatever monies that you personally have contributed to your defined contribution retirement plan go with you. And, if you're a fully vested employee, all the money your employer contributed to your retirement plan will move too. If you're not fully vested, the amount of your employer's contributions that will move with you will depend upon your company's vesting schedule.

There are three different ways monies in your defined contribution retirement benefit packages can be handled when you're changing jobs:

1. The monies are given to you through a lump-sum distribution.

2. They are placed into a new retirement plan via a rollover.

3. They stay as they are, with your old employer.

Because all retirement plans have at least one big tax advantage—namely, you don't have to pay any income tax on the money that has accumulated in them until that money is taken out—make sure to do a trustee-to-trustee rollover to keep the tax-deferred status of your retirement plan ongoing when a distribution is made.

As was pointed out earlier, a rollover isn't what you've taught Rover to do. It means taking money from one retirement account and investing it in another without incurring any penalties.

Who Regulates? The IRC and ERISA regulate through the Internal Revenue Service and the Department of Labor.

Who Makes the Investment Selections? Both you and your employer are responsible for investment selections. First, it's the employer who presents the different kinds of investment choices to 401(k) participants. Then, once employees know what their investment choices are, it's up to them to do the selecting. That means the onus of how much your 401(k) retirement funds tally up to when it comes time to retire is actually in your hands. If investing is intimidating to you, think about the 401(k) investment selections your employer offers like this: your company is a restaurant and you've got to decide where to invest your retirement dollars based on the menu that they've made available. And don't forget: If you don't like how your investment choices are performing, most plans will allow you to redirect the money. Usually that can be done once a year.

To learn more about your firm's 401(k) plans, ask your boss to direct you to the person who handles employee benefits in your company.

403(b)s

This employee-sponsored retirement plan is available to those who work for certain nonprofit or charitable organizations such as schools, hospitals, churches, and social welfare agencies.

There are two types of 403(b) plans. The first is called a "section 403(b) pension plan" and is similar to the 401(k) in that it's a payroll reduction program. Employees using 403(b)s usually can't contribute more than 5 percent of their annual salary to it. The employer may also contribute a fixed percentage of salary to those participating in this plan.

The second kind of 403(b) is called a "tax-deferred annuity" (TDA).

Like any other kind of tax-deferred investment, taxes aren't paid on TDAs until the monies from them are drawn out.

Who Can Participate? Anyone working for certain nonprofit companies or organizations offering this plan can participate in it. Some examples of participants might be teachers, doctors, and hospital employees.

Some Pluses

1. Choices: 403(b)s may offer a broad selection of investment products to invest into, including annuities and mutual funds.
2. Taxes on both the employer's and your contributions—and the earnings from the investment—are deferred until distributions are taken.

Some Minuses

1. Performance: Because the investment performance of these plans depends upon factors such as what products you've invested into, market conditions, and the length of the investment, knowing exactly how much money you'll receive from a 403(b) plan can be difficult to calculate prior to retirement.
2. Like 401(k)s, you'll still be paying Social Security tax, and possibly state taxes, if applicable, on the full amount of your wages.

Who Regulates? The IRC and ERISA regulate through the Internal Revenue Service and the Department of Labor.

Who Makes the Investment Selections? You and your company are responsible for investment selections, just as with 401(k) plans. It's up to your company to provide you with a choice as to where your 403(b) retirement monies can be invested. Then it's your choice as to where those dollars are invested.

To learn more about 403(b)s, ask your boss to direct you to the person at your company who handles employee benefits.

457 Plans

Designed for state and local government agencies and nonprofit organizations, this retirement program is also a payroll-deduction plan, although not a particularly popular one. The Employee Benefit Research Institute (EBRI) cites a couple of reasons interest in these retirement accounts is low: public employees often have modest salaries and there are no matching contributions from employers in this plan.

Again, you won't have to pay income tax on the monies contributed to this plan until a later date. And, for the year 1995, the maximum contribution to a 457 is the lesser of $7500 a year or one-third of your annual salary. These caps can change from year to year.

Who Can Participate?   The 457 plans are offered to those working for state and local government agencies and nonprofit organizations.

Some Pluses

1. Typically, a variety of investment choices are available in 457 plans, as in other qualified retirement plans.
2. Taxes don't have to be paid on the contributions but are due when the money is withdrawn.

Some Minuses

1. There usually are no matching contributions from employers in these plans.
2. While it's the employee who contributes to this program, the employer has control over those assets.

Who Regulates?   The IRC and ERISA regulate through the Internal Revenue Service and the Department of Labor.

Who Makes the Investment Selections?   How well your retirement monies perform depends upon the investment choices you make, if choices are provided by the employer. So boning up on the investment world and having a working knowledge of how different investments—like stocks, bonds, and mutual funds—work is the best way to take advantage of this retirement plan.

For more information on 457 plans, see the employee benefits coordinator in your office.

Individual Retirement Accounts (IRAs)

IRAs have been a part of the retirement arena for over 20 years. In 1974, Congress established IRAs as a way for the millions of individuals who weren't covered by an employer-sponsored retirement plan to save for their retirement. Today any full- or part-time wage earner who is under the age of 70½ can open an IRA. The maximum amount anyone can contribute to an IRA is currently $2000 per year or, if you're married and have a nonworking spouse, $2250. Because IRAs are so popular, Chapter 6 is devoted to this subject. There you'll find answers to some of the most frequently asked questions about IRAs. Before turning to that chapter, remember that IRAs are the vessel into which investments and investment products are placed. They are *not* stand-alone investments.

Who Can Participate?   Any wage earner, nonworking spouse of an employee, or nonworking divorced person receiving qualified alimony may open an IRA.

Some Pluses

1. The IRA audience is a large one. Even people who already have a retirement plan through their employer can open an IRA.
2. All money invested in an IRA grows tax-deferred until the time it's taken out, even though the money used to fund the IRA may or may not be tax deductible in the calendar year in which it was made.
3. Opening an IRA is generally inexpensive. You may open new IRAs annually and even contribute to that account monthly if you'd like to.

Some Minuses

1. The penalties for early withdrawals can be costly. There may also be penalties imposed for late withdrawals and for withdrawing too much money out of an IRA annually.
2. Make sure to put a lid on the number of separate IRAs you own. IRAs frequently come with fees and charges, which impact investment performance. So even though it's okay to open a new IRA annually, be careful not to have too many different accounts and be sure to consolidate your IRAs whenever possible. Also, keep tabs on which IRAs you've opened with tax-deductible monies and which you've opened with after-tax monies. Confusing the two can create additional paperwork headaches once you begin withdrawing that money.

Who Regulates?   The Internal Revenue Code regulates IRAs.

Who Makes the Investment Selections?   You and only you are responsible for investment selections. The "I" in IRA stands for "individual" and it is all up to you to learn about IRAs and to familiarize yourself with the kinds of investment opportunities these accounts can provide you with during your retirement years.

To learn more about IRAs, refer to Chapter 6, or ask your broker, banker, financial planner, or insurance representative to provide you with information about them. Or call the IRS and ask them for their free booklet about IRAs, number 590. (The phone numbers are 1-800-TAX-FORM and 1-800-829-3676.)

Keoghs

Keogh plans are named after U.S. Rep. Eugene J. Keogh of New York who sponsored the legislation creating these plans through the Self-Employed Individuals Tax Retirement Act of 1962. Keoghs, like Simplified Employee Pension Individual Retirement Accounts (SEP-IRAs), were created so the self-employed could provide pensions for themselves and their employees. Keoghs are tax-deferred plans which can be either defined contribution plans or defined benefit plans or both.

Like all tax-deferred retirement plans, there is a penalty for the early withdrawal of any money accumulated in a Keogh account and for monies left in them too long—after age $70\frac{1}{2}$. The maximum yearly contributions one can make into a Keogh plan depend upon whether it's a defined benefit or defined contribution plan. For example, in a money-purchase Keogh, the maximum that can be contributed each year is currently $30,000, or 25 percent of one's net earned income. In a profit-sharing Keogh, the most that can be added each year is $30,000 or 13.04 percent of one's net earned income.

Defined benefit Keoghs allow the largest amounts of monies to be contributed annually. But there is a difference between the maximum amount of money that the self-employed are allowed to contribute annually versus the limit caps the employed may contribute. The rules here are tricky, so be sure to check with your tax advisor for the particulars.

As in other defined benefit retirement plans, when the time comes to take the money out, your choices may be to take a one-time lump-sum distribution or to receive the monies periodically as you would from an annuity. (An annuity is a life insurance investment product that pays a monthly, quarterly, semiannual, or annual income to those investing in it.)

Who Can Participate?   The self-employed—like farmers, small business owners, freelance consultants, independent contractors, sole proprietors, and members of business partnerships along with their employees—may all open Keogh accounts.

Some Pluses

1. Keoghs provide the self-employed—and their employees—with an excellent retirement planning opportunity. As with IRAs, SEP-IRAs, and some 401(k)s, the choices as to where one's retirement dollars can be invested may be quite broad. Depending upon legal parameters, one may then be as aggressive or as conservative as one wishes with investment choices.

2. High-income earners, like doctors or lawyers with their own private practices, often find Keoghs appealing because of the large amounts of money they can invest into them each year.

3. You may open an IRA along with a Keogh. Having one doesn't prohibit you from also opening the other. Whether the money invested in the IRA can be fully tax deductible, however, will depend upon your annual income.

Some Minuses

1. They are expensive. Defined benefit Keoghs may be expensive to fund and to administer. Defined contribution Keoghs are less costly to create.

2. Knowing exactly where and how to invest your Keogh money is often the biggest hurdle facing anybody with a say as to where their retirement dollars go.

3. Remember, like IRAs, Keoghs are instruments used in retirement planning. They are not investments themselves.

Who Regulates?   The IRC and ERISA through the Internal Revenue Service and the Labor Department.

Who Makes the Investment Selections?   You do. Keogh's are for the self- employed and their employees.

To learn more about Keoghs, ask your broker, financial advisor, or certified public accountant. Or write to the IRS and request booklet numbers 535 and 560.

Money-Purchase Plans

In these defined contribution plans, which can also be one type of Keogh, the employer is the one who must add to his employee's retirement account. And he must add a specific percentage of the employee's compensation each and every year.

Who Can Participate?   Anyone employed by a company offering a money-purchase plan may participate in it.

Some Pluses

1. Your employer is the one committed to contributing a fixed percentage of your wages to this plan each year. That means, this isn't a salary-reduction program that you can contribute to. Once your employer creates a money-purchase plan, he must contribute the stated percentage of wages annually as outlined by the program.

2. Employees can benefit from these plans if the monies are successfully invested.

Some Minuses

1. To get at this money you have to be separated from service with the company. The size of your pension then depends on your length of service and your company's vesting schedule.

2. Like all defined contribution plans, there's a market risk and hence no guarantee of how successfully your retirement monies will be invested.

3. Currently the maximum an employer can contribute to a money-purchase plan is 25 percent of that employee's annual salary or no more than $30,000 per year per employee. If the company offering a money-purchase plan is unable to make these annual contributions, it could face a stiff penalty and have to pay a tax of 10 percent to Uncle Sam for any funding deficiencies.

Who Regulates?   The IRC and ERISA regulate through the Internal Revenue Service and the Labor Department.

Who Makes the Investment Selections?   The employer is responsible for investment selections.

To learn more about money-purchase plans ask your boss to direct you to the person at your company who handles employee benefits for your firm.

Profit-Sharing Plans

The oldest of the defined contribution plans, profit-sharing plans are qualified plans that have been around for well over 100 years. Some of the first companies to institute them for their employees were Pillsbury Mills, Procter & Gamble, and Harris Trust & Savings Bank in Chicago. According to the U.S. Department of Labor, in 1993 there were about 3.8 million, or 13 percent, full-time employees participating in profit-sharing plans.

There are three different kinds of profit-sharing plans available: the cash plan (which is not a qualified plan), the deferred plan, and the combination plan. In a cash plan, once the company's profits are determined, contributions are paid out to the employee in the form of cash, checks, or stock. These contributions are then taxed as ordinary income in the year in which the employee receives them.

Deferred plans are the most popular profit-sharing plans. They work like this: benefits from these plans are put into employee accounts where the money is invested but not distributed until a later date. Taxes on these accounts, as in other qualified retirement plans, aren't due until the funds are distributed.

In a combination plan, employees have some choices. They can either defer all, or a portion of, the profit-sharing allocations each year. This means that the portion of the allocation that gets deferred will be left to accumulate tax-deferred until a later date and the portion that gets taken in cash will have taxes levied on it in the calendar year in which those monies were received.

Who Can Participate?   Employees of companies offering profit-sharing plans may participate in them.

Some Pluses

1. Sharing in the success of one's company can be very profitable. And often the greater the company profits, the bigger your piece of the profit-sharing pie can be.

2. Along with all tax-deferred benefits, more and more companies are offering choices about where the monies in these plans may be invested.

Some Minuses

1. If your profit-sharing plan pays you in cash, be careful not to spend it. Invest it by creating a retirement plan, like an IRA, for yourself.

2. Not all companies have profits to share.

Who Regulates?   The IRC and ERISA regulate through the Internal Revenue Service and the Labor Department.

Who Makes the Investment Selections? Your employer is responsible for the investment selection. But, in this case, the company has to have earned profits before any can be shared. So, think about supplementing a profit-sharing plan with another tax-deferred plan. One you've set up on your own—like an IRA, or a SEP-IRA, or an annuity.

To learn more about profit-sharing plans, ask your boss to direct you to the person handling employee benefits at your company.

Simplified Employee Pension Individual Retirement Accounts (SEP-IRAs)

SEP-IRAs have been around since 1979. Like Keoghs they were created to give the self-employed, the small business owner, and the small business owner's employees a simple, low-cost, tax-advantaged way to save for their retirement. In these very basic retirement plans, the employer makes the annual contributions to the IRA accounts of his or her employees. Then, by March 15 of each year, the employer must tell each employee how much money was contributed to his or her account.

Unlike Keoghs, SEP-IRAs are an inexpensive way for an employer to offer his employees a retirement plan. That's because the employees own and manage their own accounts, so the employer has no administrative costs, only contribution expenses.

The maximum contribution an employer may make into a SEP-IRA is currently capped at 15 percent of each employee's annual wage or $22,500, whichever is less.

Who Can Participate? The self-employed—for example, farmers, small business owners, freelancers, consultants, independent contractors, sole proprietors, and anyone earning any amount of self-employed income—may open SEP-IRAs. Someone who works, say, for a corporation during the day and has a part-time at-home business that provides her with an additional income, could in effect participate in a variety of retirement plans, including the one her daytime employer offers and the SEP-IRA she sets up for herself. Corporate employers may also sponsor SEP-IRA accounts for their employees.

Some Pluses

1. SEP-IRAs are an efficient, cost-effective way to provide the small business owner and his employees with a retirement program.

2. Because your employer makes the yearly contributions, you won't have to ante-up any of your own salary to fund this plan. And, depending upon the size of the company you work for, there may also be a salary-reduction arrangement available to you.

3. Deciding where your retirement money is invested in this plan is your responsibility. This again is good news for those who know something about the investment arena, and bad news for those unwilling to learn about investing. So the opportunities for where your retirement dollars can be invested are almost endless. Consequently, you may be as aggressive or as conservative with those monies as you'd like to be.

4. If you work for someone providing a SEP-IRA, you may also open your own IRA independent of the SEP-IRA.

Some Minuses

1. Knowing exactly where or how to invest one's retirement money is a big challenge. So, before plunking down your retirement dollars into just any investment, know what you're getting into. After all, it's your money—and your future—that you're hoping to fund.

2. Although great for the small business owner, SEP-IRAs aren't for the big guys. Business owners can sock away the most money in a defined benefit Keogh.

Who Regulates?   The IRC and ERISA regulate through the Internal Revenue Service and the Labor Department.

Who Makes the Investment Selections?   Again, it's up to your boss to offer this opportunity, but it's you who chooses how the money in this plan gets invested.

To learn more about SEP-IRAs: If you're employed, ask your employer for more-detailed information about how these retirement plans work. If you're self-employed ask your broker, financial advisor, or CPA for more information. And write or call the IRS asking for a copy of their booklet on SEP-IRAs, number 590. Their toll-free number is 1-800-TAX-FORM.

Tax-Sheltered Annuities

Tax-sheltered annuities (TSAs) are investment products brought to us from the insurance industry. TSAs, also called Section 457s, are available as a retirement plan only to teachers and other employees of tax-exempt organizations. (Be careful not to confuse TSAs with the fixed and/or variable annuity. The latter are investment products offering tax-deferred investing opportunities to individual investors and are purchased with after-tax dollars.)

In TSAs the employees, not the employer, make annual contributions to the plan.

Basically a TSA is a mutual fund with a few extra twists. One of those twists is more costs. Because any investment product the insurance industry brings to market must have some kind of death benefit attached to it (a guaranteed death benefit is what grants an annuity the right to be a tax-deferred investment), there are additional costs for this product that a mutual fund on its own doesn't have.

Currently the cap on employee contributions to a TSA is $5000 a year, although that cap may be increased for people who have worked for a nonprofit organization for more than 15 years.

Who Can Participate?   TSAs are offered to people employed by tax-exempt and public organizations such as public education systems, churches, hospitals, and public charities.

Some Pluses

1. The monies in these accounts compound and grow tax-deferred until the time that they are taken out.

2. TSAs can be one of the many products used to create your retirement portfolio.

Some Minuses

1. Because of the added cost of things like mortality expense ratios and administrative fees—on top of which the annual mutual fund expense fees are added—monies invested into TSAs have to work harder in performance to overcome these built-in annual costs.

2. These can be very low-yielding investments with high initial and ongoing fees.

Who Regulates?   The IRC and ERISA regulate through the Internal Revenue Service and the Labor Department.

Who Makes the Investment Selections?   Your employer selects the annuity products it wants to offer. Then it's up to you to invest, and the market to provide the performance results.

For more information about TSAs, ask your boss to direct you to the person in charge of employee benefits at your school, company, or nonprofit organization.

Thrift or Savings Plans

Thrift or savings plans are defined contribution plans in which the employees add their own money into their own retirement coffers.

Workers using these retirement vehicles can make contributions to them either via basic payroll-deduction contributions (some companies even match contributions here) or through individual contributions in which funds aren't matched. Popular investment choices for money earmarked for thrift or savings plans include things like guaranteed investment contracts (GICs), mutual funds, and company stock.

All income from thrift plans grows tax-deferred until the monies are withdrawn. In 1995 the caps on how much money can be contributed to any individual account in a thrift or savings plan topped off at $30,000 per year or not more than 25 percent of one's annual salary.

Who Can Participate?   Employees of any organization offering this kind of retirement opportunity may participate in it.

Some Pluses

1. Thrift plans, like other defined contribution plans, generally offer their participants a choice as to where their retirement monies can be invested. This, in turn, allows employees to invest their retirement dollars as aggressively or as conservatively as they wish.
2. After-tax employee contributions, unlike 401(k) contributions, may be withdrawn without a penalty, provided you've been in the plan for at least two years.

Some Minuses

1. Depending upon the company, the choice of thrift or savings plan investments may be limited.
2. Employers are under no obligation to make contributions to these plans.

Who Regulates?   The IRC and ERISA regulate under the direction of the Internal Revenue Service and the Labor Department.

Who Makes the Investment Selections?   You are responsible for the investment selections.

For more information on thrift and savings plans, see the person in charge of employee benefits at the company you work for.

GETTING STUNG: TWICE

As terrific an opportunity as investing into IRAs and SEP-IRAs or Keoghs can be, don't put all of your money into retirement plans. You could wind up in a financial bind and need to use the money in these qualified retirement plans before you have reached age 59½.

John Howley, an accountant in Lake Worth, Florida, warns his clients against putting too much money into qualified retirement accounts and not keeping enough money in easy-to-get-at places like their ordinary savings or money-market accounts.

"I can't tell you the number of times my clients have opted for an IRA instead of keeping an ordinary savings account—and then wind up without any emergency money when they need it."

Pouring all of your disposable cash into a retirement account is akin to putting all your eggs in one basket; it's a practice that's never made good economic sense. And it's one that can cost you.

How? Look at it like this: Just pretend you're in the 28 percent tax bracket, need to withdraw $2000 from your IRA for an emergency—say, to pay for tuition for little Alex's preschool, or for the new air conditioner you need all of a sudden.

Getting at that IRA money is going to cost a bundle. First, there will be the 10 percent IRS penalty for early withdrawal from the IRA. That penalty will cost a quick $200 if you're withdrawing $2000. And then there's the tax that you'll have to pay on that additional $2000 in income you just received. Which in your tax bracket, will amount to $560. (And if that $2000 bumps your income up into another bracket, it could cost even more!)

So, of the $2000 you withdrew, $760 was eaten up in new taxes, leaving you $1240 to spend.

The moral of this story is, no matter what age—or stage—you're at in life, it's just as important to have easily accessible money as it is to have established a retirement plan. Because emergencies always happen, be prepared. Part of a good savings plan includes money stashed away for short-, intermediate-, and long-term goals. Make sure to keep some cash at your immediate disposal to cover life's many surprises.

Most experts suggest building an emergency fund totaling 3 to 6 months of your living expenses. Others extend that savings pot out to 1 or 2 years depending upon your career and family needs. If you're uncertain as to what size your emergency fund ought to be, try using $5000 as a beginning goal and adjust that figure upward or downward according to your personal needs.

6
Individual Retirement Accounts (IRAs)

Question: Why should I open an IRA?

Answer: Individual retirement accounts are wonderful tax-deferred investment vehicles available to millions of working and nonworking Americans. In fact, for a large percentage of those who invest the maximum yearly amount into an IRA (currently $2000 for individuals and $2250 for couples with a nonworking spouse), the contribution is tax deductible. But IRAs make sense even if your annual contribution into one isn't tax deductible. So, don't overlook IRAs just because you (1) don't understand how they work, (2) don't think you have enough money to invest into one, or (3) have to fund it with after-tax dollars.

An IRA's biggest drawing card is in the opportunity this retirement vehicle provides for money to grow and compound tax-deferred. It's the combination of choosing various investments to fund your IRA, along with the magic of compounding that makes this retirement plan appealing.

To *fund* means to buy an investment for your IRA. For example, if you buy 100 shares of *xyz* stock for your IRA account, you would say that your IRA has been funded with *xyz* stock. Or, if you invest $500 into the AIM Weingarten Fund, you would say that your IRA has been funded by that mutual fund.

Question: Once I open an IRA, in subsequent years am I locked into using the same investment vehicle I opened the account with?

Answer: You can fund an IRA differently each year. Every single year brings new investment opportunities for the individual retirement account investor. That means a certificate of deposit from your local bank isn't the only investment product you can invest retirement monies into, or that your bank isn't the only place to open an IRA.

The choices of what kinds of products to put your IRA money into range from mutual funds to individual stocks, bonds, bank CDs, and even collectibles. So don't feel that you're "stuck" once you've opened an IRA. You're not. Monies in these accounts can be placed into a variety of different products, traded or sold, and in the case of mutual funds, exchanged among the mutual funds within a fund family.

Here's an example: Let's say that this year you have $1000 to invest in an IRA and have decided to put that money into one of the Janus family of mutual funds, selecting The Janus Fund.

When next year rolls around and you've got another $1000 earmarked for your retirement, it's your call as to whether or not you choose to invest again in The Janus Fund. You're not automatically required to do so. If bonds look more attractive that year because of favorable interest rates, you may invest that $1000 in a bond fund or an individual bond.

Having new money to invest year after year for your retirement means making new investment decisions each year. These investment decisions allow you to diversify where and how your retirement monies get invested.

Question: Do I need $2000 to open an IRA?

Answer: You don't need $2000 to open an IRA. That's currently the *maximum* any one person can contribute to an IRA annually. Often only a couple of hundred dollars is enough to get this retirement account started.

The minimum amount of money required to fund an IRA often depends upon how much money you've got to invest and the investment product chosen. Mutual funds are a great way to fund IRAs. And many mutual fund families give investors an opportunity to open an IRA with as little as $250. Lots of people fund their IRAs with certificates of deposit because minimum investments there can be as little as $100. Funding your IRA with individual stocks or corporate bonds often requires more money, like one or two thousand dollars.

Question: Do I have to contribute to my IRA every year?

Answer: Once you've opened an IRA you don't have to contribute to it each and every year. But that account does stay open until you start withdrawing money from it, which means there will probably be fees that need to be paid annually for that account.

Question: How much can I earn each year and still receive an income tax deduction for my IRA contribution?

Answer: For the answer to that question take a look at Table 6-1 on the following page.

Basically, single people earning $25,000 or less per year, and married couples filing jointly who earn $40,000 or less per year may deduct all of their IRA contribution money from their taxable income.

Question: Will I have to pay fees and/or administrative costs on my IRA account?

Answer: There's a price for everything. Even on retirement accounts.

Fees are typically charged to IRA investors in one of three places. They are when opening an IRA account, when funding it, and then for the annual maintenance of that account.

The fees for initially opening an IRA may be waived, may be as little as $10 or $15, or may be much higher and based upon the dollar amount invested into the account. The reasons companies charge fees to open IRAs is to cover the cost of handling them and to pay for the work involved in maintaining them.

Some brokerage firms and mutual fund families waive all fees associated with the opening of and the maintenance of IRAs provided that the account balances are over $5000 or $10,000. Others don't. It pays to shop around.

Table 6-1. Current IRA Eligibility Test

Adjusted gross income			You or spouse covered by pension plan?	Type of contribution ($2000 maximum)
Married, filing:				
Jointly	Separately	Individual		
$40,000 or under	$0	$25,000 or under	Yes	Fully deductible
$40,000 or under	$0	$25,000 or under	No	Fully deductible
Between $40,000 and $50,000	Less than $10,000	Between $25,000 and $35,000	Yes	Partially deductible
Between $40,000 and $50,000	Less than $10,000	Between $25,000 and $35,000	No	Fully deductible
$50,000 or over	$10,000 or over	$35,000 or over	Yes	Nondeductible
$50,000 or over	$10,000 or over	$35,000 or over	No	Fully deductible

SOURCE: Employee Benefit Research Institute, *Fundamentals of Employee Benefit Programs*, Fourth Edition.

Funding your IRA often means spending some money on commissions—like the ones required when buying shares of stock to put in an IRA, or those imposed on bonds or on shares of mutual funds that have sales charges. Don't forget, mutual fund investors will also have annual fees to pay on the funds they've invested into each year too.

All of these fees added together can take a big bite out of an IRA's overall performance—especially if the balance in it is only a few hundred dollars. For example, when I did a minisurvey of IRA fees in January of 1994, here's what I found: If you're a fan of the Twentieth Century funds, this no-load fund family had a $10 per year per fund fee on their IRAs. But that fee gets capped at $30 per year. That means, if you had opened an IRA and funded it one year by investing in, say, the Twentieth Century Ultra Fund, opened another IRA the next year funding it with their Balanced Fund and so on until in five years you had five different IRA accounts there, the most your annual IRA maintenance fee would be is $30. But, if your IRA balance totaled more than $10,000, in one or all accounts, that fee would be waived. But, even though the annual IRA fee may get waived, you'll still have annual maintenance charges to pay on the individual funds you've invested into.

Over at Fidelity, it was a different story. Because Fidelity plays two roles for investors—that of a brokerage firm as well as that of a fund family—the IRA fees are more complicated. There you would have to pay a $10 annual fee for an IRA Mutual Fund Account if the account balance is under $5000. You would pay nothing if it were over that amount. If, however, you funded your IRA with one of the many Fidelity funds that carries a 3 percent load, you wouldn't have to pay that load—except if you chose to invest into the Fidelity Magellan Fund, Fidelity New Millennium Fund, and the Fidelity Select Portfolios. But, if you open a Fidelity self-directed IRA, the annual maintenance fee is $20 per year on account balances under $5000. Whew! Complicated, isn't it?

Quick & Reilly, a full-service discount brokerage firm, keeps things simpler. At this brokerage house in January 1994 you had to pay $25 a year to maintain an IRA if the balance in it was under $10,000. And you paid nothing if it was over. Plus, there were various commission charges to pay—like the load on a mutual fund or commissions on individual stocks or bonds used to fund the IRA. (A "load" is the fee charged on broker-sold mutual funds.)

At Smith Barney, annual IRA maintenance fees at that time were $40 per year, whether you had $500 in your IRA or $1 million. Plus you'd pay whatever commissions necessary, depending upon the products you funded the IRA with.

At Merrill Lynch, the minimum annual fees for IRAs in January 1994 were $35 dollars a year—the maximum, $100. Here again, if you chose to fund that IRA with a mutual fund, there would be that fund's load fees along with the annual IRA expense that have to be paid plus that fund's annual maintenance fees. Other investment products you chose would also carry their own annual fee structures.

"Don't forget, time is your greatest ally when it comes to achieving your retirement goals," says Rowena Itchon, a spokesperson at T. Rowe Price. By the way, their IRA annual fees run $10 per year per account unless the balance is over $5000. In that case, the fees are waived.

So before you open an IRA, make sure to ask:

- How much does this IRA account cost to open?
- What will the annual charges on the IRA be?
- What kinds of fees, commissions, and/or sales charges will I have to pay to fund my IRA?
- What kinds of annual maintenance fees will I have to pay each year on the products I've funded my IRA with?
- What is the least amount of money I can invest into the products I want to fund my account with?

For your information, buying and holding individual stocks or bonds in an IRA might be the least expensive way to fund one. You'll only have to pay commissions on each when buying and when selling. So, if you don't trade any of these securities within a year, the only IRA fee would be the one imposed on that account.

Question: Is my IRA money federally insured by the Federal Deposit Insurance Corporation (FDIC)?

Answer: That depends on how you've invested the money.

If your IRA investments at the bank are in mutual funds, those monies aren't insured. But if you've invested in certificates of deposit (CDs) or that bank's money-market deposit account, that money would be insured if the bank carried FDIC insurance. And, beginning December 19, 1993, the FDIC put an insurance cap of $100,000 on all monies held in retirement accounts.

FDIC-insured banks provide insurance coverage for deposits in four different account categories: individual, joint, retirement, and trust. In each category the FDIC insurance cap is $100,000.

Because understanding FDIC insurance coverage can be tricky, look for a copy of "Your Insured Deposits" in your bank's lobby. Or write to the FDIC (550 17th Street, Washington, D.C. 20429) directly to obtain a free copy of that pamphlet. While you're at it, ask for another one titled "Insured or Not Insured."

Question: What are the penalties for early IRA withdrawal?

Answer: IRA monies cannot be withdrawn without penalty until you reach age 59½. Any money pulled before then will be subject to a 10 percent IRS penalty. To add salt to that penalty wound, all monies withdrawn are always added to your annual income and could mean you've got more income tax to pay in the year in which the money was taken out. So an early IRA withdrawal could cost you plenty.

Here's an example of how that might work: If you pull $10,000 out of your IRA and you're age 50, you'll have to pay Uncle Sam $1000 in penalties on that money, thanks to the 10 percent penalty for early withdrawal before age 59½. That leaves you with $9000. Then, the full $10,000 gets added to your tax return in the form of ordinary income in the year it's received. And, if you're real unlucky, that early withdrawal move could not only boost up your annual income but could mean that some of your income gets taxed at a higher tax bracket. Ouch!

So, early withdrawal of IRA monies can knock out a lot of the yolk of your retirement nest egg. If you don't want to see a goodly portion of your retirement savings paid out in taxes, (1) try your best not to withdraw any money, even though that may seem tempting, and (2) follow the rules. This money has been earmarked for your retirement. Let it work for you.

Question: Are there any penalties for leaving money in an IRA for too long?

Answer: Make sure to begin taking income out from your IRA account by April 1 of the year *after the year* you reach age 70½. If you don't do that, you'll have to pay some hefty penalties. It works like this: If your seventieth birthday is on June 28, 1994, on December 28 of that year you'll be 70½ and that means you must begin taking money out of your IRA account by April of 1995, to avoid paying a penalty.

According to the Employee Benefit Research Institute, minimum IRA distributions not taken by April 1 of the calendar year following the year in which you turn 70½ are subject to a 50 percent excise tax.

Calculations for how much money you have to withdraw before that time depend upon a couple of things; how much money there is in your IRA and your life expectancy from the IRS's point of view.

You can also be hit with a 15 percent penalty for withdrawing *too much* money from your IRA. Thus, to avoid unnecessary penalties for withdrawing money too late or withdrawing too much money, be sure to check with your tax advisor to fully understand the regulations.

Question: What can I fund my IRA with?

Answer: There are about as many different ways to fund an IRA as there are different brands of cereal. To get an inkling of how extensive a list that is, just think about the choices there are as you walk down the cereal aisle of your local supermarket. In fact, it's easier to point out the things you can't fund an IRA with than it is the things you can.

For the record, here's a list of the collectibles that you currently may *not* fund your IRA account with:

Art

Antiques

Rugs

Stamps

Wines

Coins—other than certain U.S. minted gold or silver coins and state-issued coins circulated after November 10, 1988.

Legal but poor IRA investment choices include tax-free bonds and shares of a tax-free municipal bond fund.

Remember, an IRA is a conduit in which investments placed inside of it won't incur a tax consequence until a later date. The reasons tax-exempt investments don't make sense for IRAs is because they already have a tax advantage, they are tax-exempt! Putting a tax-exempt investment product into a tax-deferred vehicle like an IRA is like putting on one raincoat and then another right on top of it. It doesn't make sense, or keep you any drier.

Common IRA investments that do benefit from the tax-deferred opportunities of IRA investing include individual stocks and bonds, a host of mutual funds, and CDs.

Before buying any product for an IRA make sure to check its past performance history. Although past performance is no indication of what the future might hold, it does offer clues as to how an investment has previously worked and how it has performed under various market conditions.

If you'd like to buy shares of individual stocks for your IRA, for instance, take the time to find out some basics. Learn about what the company makes or produces, check to see how well the stock has performed since it began, find out if it currently does or ever has paid a dividend, and look at its balance sheet. Books like *Value Line* and *Standard & Poor's Stock Guide* are chock full of this kind of data and can be found in the reference section at most libraries.

Those interested in mutual funds can use reference books such as *Mutual Fund Values*; *Mutual Fund Sourcebook*; *Standard & Poor's/Lipper Mutual Fund Profiles*; and *The Thomas J. Herzfeld Encyclopedia of Closed-End Funds* to learn more about the performance history of different kinds of mutual funds. Individual corporate-bond investors can look at one of Moody's Investment Services' books or the *Standard & Poor's Bond Guide.*

As always, the more you know about a product before investing in it, the better your chances are of making some wise investment decisions and being satisfied with that product's performance.

Question: How liquid will the investments in my IRA be?

Answer: When it comes time to cash in your IRA investments, how quickly you'll be able to get at that money will depend on the investments that you've made.

Selling shares of a mutual fund, like the selling of most common stocks, can be done on any business day of the year. But selling some preferred shares of stock—that might not be traded daily on the stock exchange—could take more time. It can also take more than one day to sell shares of some limited partnerships or foreign securities. Even some individual bonds can't always be liquidated in one day.

Ask your broker or financial advisor about the liquidity of the products with which you've funded your IRA before investing to get an accurate idea of how soon you'll be able to have that retirement cash in your hands.

Question: What are the risks of the investments typically used to fund an IRA?

Answer: Making investments and taking risks go hand in hand. If you're a stock market investor, history has shown that the longer one holds on to a stock the better the chances are for that stock to go up in value. But not all stocks make people money.

History also shows us that bonds, too, make money in time. Selling a bond before it matures, however, may or may not return to you your original investment. Real estate has made some investors millionaires. And it has cost others their fortunes.

Investing doesn't come with any written financial guarantees. If there were to be one, it might read: Buyer beware!

Learn about the risks involved with any product before investing in it. And keep in mind that financial fortunes aren't made overnight.

Question: Are there any reasons *not* to open an IRA?

Answer: Yes. Even though IRAs make good sense for lots of people, they aren't for everyone. And, depending upon the amount of money used to open an account, the investments chosen, the return on those investments, the length of time the money stays invested, and the costs associated with keeping the retirement account going, it's possible that building a retirement nest egg *outside* of an IRA could be the smartest move.

It doesn't make a lot of sense to open an IRA if you're just a few years away from retirement. Nor does it make sense to have too many IRAs or to keep them if the annual expenses on them is running higher than the returns.

For instance, if you're in your late 60s, these tax-deferred retirement products may save some money on your tax bill, but because the law requires people to start withdrawing money from their IRAs by age $70\frac{1}{2}$, that limited time frame might not give the money invested much chance to grow and compound tax deferred, particularly if there were commissions or loads on the investment products. A wiser tax-deferred investment alternative in such a case might be a variable or fixed annuity. In many annuities the proceeds don't have to be taken out until age 80 or 85. So for the mature investor wanting tax-deferred investment opportunities make sure to take a good look at how long you intend to have monies invested before opening an IRA.

Having too many IRAs isn't a good idea either. Not only could that be a bookkeeping nightmare, but too many IRAs can be costly.

Ten different IRAs at 10 different mutual fund families in which each fund family is charging an annual IRA maintenance fee of $10 a year means a portion of your fund's yield is being eaten up by fees. How big that fee bite is depends upon the size of the balances in each account. So consolidate these accounts whenever possible.

Retirement Planning Tip _____

According to Fidelity Investments, money invested in IRAs is deductible for an estimated 50 million Americans not covered by other types of pension plans or falling within certain income categories. If you've overlooked this retirement plan vehicle, it might be time to reconsider.

7
Social Security

If you're counting on Social Security to provide retirement income to live on, you're probably in for an unpleasant surprise.

A Little History

To set the record straight, the pension benefits retirees receive from Social Security, as prescribed in the Social Security Act of 1935, were never intended to be an individual's only source of income during his or her retirement years. That money was originally designed to provide a helping hand for those in need.

The broad scope of that act, which brought things such as Social Security retirement benefits, social insurance, and public assistance and welfare services into existence in 1937 has, through the years, moved from a "service" kind of government program into an "entitlement"—one which masses of people have come to depend upon.

Some of the social insurance programs within the Social Security Act include income benefits for retirement; survivors and disability insurance, called Old Age and Survivors Insurance and Disability Insurance (OASDI); unemployment insurance; and hospital and medical insurance for the aged and the disabled. So, along with providing retirees with Social Security income and Medicare benefits, this act also provides benefits to people who may or may not be retired but who are disabled, dependents of someone receiving Social Security, widows, widowers, or children of someone who has died.

Who Qualifies?

To receive retirement income from Social Security benefits, FICA taxes need to be paid. In addition, to qualify for benefits you must have acquired the appropriate number of "quarters of coverage." Here's how that works: quarters of coverage come your way by working "calendar quarters" and then receiving credits for them. In 1995, one calendar quarter credit was given for every $630 earned.

Calendar quarters are represented by three-month cycles in any year. The calendar quarters in a year end on March 31, June 30, September 30, and December 31. Which means, in order to obtain four quarter credits in 1995 your income would have to have been at least $2520.

The number of calendar quarters needed to be eligible for Social Security income benefits depends upon your date of birth: Those born in 1928 or before will need 39 quarters of coverage. Anyone born in 1929 or later, needs to have acquired 40 quarters for full coverage.

How much money you receive monthly as a result of paying into FICA, the Social Security tax, depends upon a mathematical formula that's calculated around your average annual earnings.

Doing the Math

Computers do all the calculating when it comes to figuring out who gets what in Social Security retirement benefits. That's a good thing. Because it would take more than 10 figures, 10 toes, and an abacus for most of us to accurately compute the five-step formula used to figure monthly income retirement benefits.

But if you'd like to give it a try, here's the formula—verbatim—showing how Social Security comes up with the amount of monthly income you'll receive.

Step 1.   First, your earnings covered by Social Security are listed starting with 1951.

Step 2.   Next, your earnings are adjusted for changes in average wages over the years. For example, average earnings for 1992 are five times greater than average earnings were for 1964. To make 1964 earnings comparable with current earnings, they are multiplied by five. Earnings are adjusted for each year up to the year you reach 60. The adjustment factor becomes smaller the closer you get to the present. After you reach age 60, actual earnings are used.

Step 3.   From this list, the highest years of earnings are selected to figure your benefits. For nearly everyone retiring now and in the future, 35 years of earnings are used to figure retirement benefits. If you haven't worked for 35 years, we'll add years of "zero" earnings to your record to total 35 years.

Step 4. The earnings for these years are totaled and divided by 420 (the number of months in 35 years) to get your average monthly earnings. This is the number used to figure your benefit rate.

Step 5. A three-level formula is applied to your average monthly earnings to arrive at an actual benefit rate. For example, for people born in 1932:

- We multiply the first $422 of your monthly earnings by 90 percent.
- We multiply the next $2123 of your earnings by 32 percent.
- We multiply any remaining amount by 15 percent.

The results are added together and rounded to the next lower dime. This is your basic full retirement age (currently 65) benefit rate.

A new formula is set each year for people reaching 62 that year. The percentages remain the same, but the dollar amounts change. Even if you don't retire until later, we'll figure your benefits using the formula based on the year you turned 62. We don't use this formula if you also get or are eligible for a pension based on work— usually a government job where you didn't pay Social Security taxes. For more information about this, ask for a copy of, "A Pension from Work Not Covered by Social Security," Publication No. 05-10045.

To give you an idea of how all this stacks up here's a look at the average Social Security monthly income benefits in 1994:

- The average retired individual received $674 a month, while the average retired couple got $1140 in monthly benefits.

- The average disabled person received $641 in monthly benefits and the average disabled individual with a spouse and a child received $1092 in monthly benefits.

- The average widow(er) received $631 in monthly benefits while the average young widow(er) with two children received $1316.

To learn about your current status and the amount of benefits, if any, you could receive from Social Security, get in touch with the Social Security Administration. Their toll-free telephone number is 1-800-772-1213.

Actual representatives are available to speak with you from 7 a.m. to 7 p.m., Monday through Friday. But feel free to call that number 24 hours a day, seven days a week. When I called, the message was a recorded one asking me to provide my name and address so information could be sent to me. The packet sent out consists of information on how one's benefits are calculated, plus a number of pamphlets on subjects ranging from Medicare to how to get Social Security checks if an individual has to be out of the United States for an extended period of time. There's also a card to send back requesting an estimate on what your individual projected benefits might be. (On the card, you'll be asked to fill in information about how many years you plan to keep working, as well as what your projected annual income will be for those years. So when filling out this card, be prepared to make some projections.)

WHERE YOUR FICA DOLLAR GOES

In 1993, here's how the money that you paid in FICA taxes got divvied up. Out of every one dollar paid in FICA taxes:

- 73 cents went into a trust fund from which Social Security monthly benefits are paid to retirees and families.
- 19 cents went into a trust fund to pay Medicare benefits.
- 8 cents went into a trust to pay disability benefits.

Social Security for the Employed

If you're close to retirement and planning on working during your retirement years, how much money you earn may affect your Social Security benefits. Limits on how much money you can earn annually before your benefits get tapped are based on your age. In 1995 those income limits were as follows:

- If you're under age 65, you can earn up to $8160 before your income benefits are affected. But for every $2 that you earn over that amount, $1 in benefits is withheld.
- For those aged 65 to 69, you can earn up to $11,280 with no reduction in Social Security income benefits, but, for every $3 earned over that amount, $1 is withheld.
- And if you're 70 years or older, you can earn as much money as you'd like. There are no income limits here. This can make working into your seventies—or beyond—very profitable.

Wealth Builder Tip _____

Currently, the best way to get the most in income benefits from Social Security is to work for at least 35 years, pay your FICA taxes all along, and earn as much money as you possibly can.

If that's too heavy a load and you'd still like to have a Social Security check delivered to your door each month after you've retired, make sure to have tallied up at least 40 quarters of credit with the Social Security Administration. Remember, to earn one credit, you've got to have made and have paid FICA tax on $630 of income within any given quarter. There are four quarters in one year.

PART 3
Demystifying Investing

8

An Overview of Investment Products

The Fear of Investing

Barbara Ballens is a 45-year-old travel writer who has had the good fortune of receiving the gift of $10,000 each year from her father. On the suggestion of his tax advisor, her dad is gifting the money to her, and she may do whatever she wants to with it.

When Barbara first started to receive the cash gift she wanted to invest it. But it took her years to be able to do so.

"I was afraid to invest the money for fear that I'd do the wrong thing with it."

The fear of investing is a common one. Particularly when you are counting on that money to "be there" in the future when you know that you're going to need it.

If you've ever had that "Gee, am I doing the right thing?" feeling when it comes to investing, keep the following in mind:

- There are no risk-free investments. All investments ask you to take some risk with the money you invest. And, risk means different things to different people. The degree of risk you take will vary from product to product. Not everyone agrees on what is and what isn't a risky investment product. Nor does everyone have the same risk appetite. Some find money risk appealing, others don't.

- Investments have risks no matter where, or from whom, you purchase them. For example, just because your bank offers an opportunity to invest through them doesn't mean the products that establishment is offering are any safer investments than the ones offered by other financial professionals.

- Investments are money products. Some investment products make their investors money, some don't. Some will suit your needs, others won't.

  To demystify the power of the word *investments*, try thinking of these money products as you would the products at your local supermarket. Walk down any aisle at your local market and the food and grocery products you pick and choose to buy are usually the ones you need—staples such as bread, eggs, toilet paper, and soap. Selecting each depends upon what your tastes and likes and dislikes are, and are based on things you've learned from your parents or through reading or advertising. Apply that very type of selection process—needs, likes, and education—to the choices of investment products. Finding the ones to suit your needs will then become simpler.

- It's your money. You are the one making the choices about how and where to spend it. Be careful not to get hoodwinked into surrendering that powerful choice. The decisions that you make about planning for your retirement are yours. And as such, they can be changed or modified whenever you feel it is appropriate.

Once Barbara realized that investing was a choice, one in which the objective was to meet her own personal needs, the whole notion of long-term financial planning became a little less intimidating—and therefore much more manageable—for her.

After Barbara began looking at her own money fears, she realized her biggest fear—that of investing the money foolishly—was overcome once she began learning more about investment products. In fact, in three years, she was able to create a diversified retirement investment portfolio for herself. One that included a savings and money-market account, individual stocks, mutual funds, IRAs, and some tax-exempt zero-coupon bonds.

"This is actually fun," she says. "I've got an awful lot to learn, but I'm miles ahead of where I was a few years ago."

Of Flowers, Vases, and Investment Products

Retirement plans, like IRAs, 401(k)s, Keoghs, and 403(b)s, are conduits, vessels into which investment products, like stocks, bonds, and mutual funds, are placed.

You might say retirement plans are a lot like a vase and the investment products we put in them like flowers coming from hundreds of different sources, all yielding something different, too. So, each vase and the flowers in it will all be different.

The following is an overview of the kinds of investment products most commonly placed into retirement account vases.

Conservative Investments

The investment products considered by most financial experts as "conservative" in nature—with the exception of good old-fashioned cash—typically pay interest to those who decide to place their money in them. They include things like savings and money-market accounts along with debt instruments like bonds.

Usually the lowest-yielding conservative interest-paying investments are savings accounts, followed by certificates of deposit (CDs) and then short-term maturing bonds, such as Treasury bills. Other than money-market accounts and savings accounts, these other conservative investments have maturity dates.

The length of time money stays in these interest-bearing investments affects the yield, that is, what you'll earn from them. One rule of thumb regarding yield is, the longer your money is invested, the higher the risks and consequently the greater the financial rewards, which is why longer-maturing securities offer investors higher returns. On the other hand, financial experts point out that low-yielding investments also have risks too; one of them is that often low yields don't keep pace with inflation. The bottom line is, even the most "conservative" investments are not without risk.

Table 8-1 breaks down conservative investment products into two categories: "dollar in, dollar out" items, which are immediately or almost immediately convertible into their face value, and investment products with maturity dates, such as CDs, savings bonds, and U.S. Treasury bills, notes, and bonds. Getting the most out of any of the latter generally means holding them until they mature.

Wealth Builder Tip_____

Conservative investments, like savings and money-market accounts, have a very definite place in a long-term investment plan. While not sexy, or hot, or razzle-dazzlely, these short-term investments often form the cornerstone from which other kinds of investment products can then be made. They are usually the first kinds of investments people make, and the ones they keep on making during the rest of their investing lives.

Table 8-1. Getting at Your Conservative Investment Products

Name of product	Type	How long	Procedure
		Dollar In, Dollar Out	
Savings account	A place to deposit money on which interest is earned.	Usually same day you need it.	Just as putting money into a savings account means filling out a deposit slip, getting money out generally requires filling out a withdrawal form, handing that over to the teller at your bank, and waiting for him or her to pass the money requested back to you.
Money-market mutual funds (MMMFs)	Money-market mutual funds are products where the shares purchased are invested into very short-term securities. MMMFs are not FDIC-insured.	Same or next-day transaction.	MMMF shares are typically bought and sold at $1 per share. Investing into money-market mutual funds requires buying shares for a dollar per share. Getting your money back more often than not means selling those shares at that same $1-per-share price.

| Money-market deposit accounts (MMDAs) | These bank mutual funds are different from MMMFs. Because MMDAs are bank products, monies invested in them are FDIC-insured up to $100,000 per account if the bank has FDIC insurance coverage. | Same-day transaction. |
| Cash | Cash, cash, glorious cash. Cash is king. Cash buys you everything, today. Right now. Instantly. There are no forms to fill out, no waiting to be done if you've got cash in hand. Cash, at your fingertips, is as liquid, i.e., as immediately available, as assets can get. | Same as above. |

(Continued)

Table 8-1. Getting at Your Conservative Investment Products (*Continued*)

Name of product	Type	How long	Procedure
		Products That Mature	
Series E or EE savings bonds	Government bonds issued at face-value denominations.		Savings bonds are sold at deep discounts. Discounts, that is, to their face value. Face value is indicated on the bond and received when that bond is cashed in on its maturity date. Because these bonds mature several years in the future, if you need to get at the money from them before the bonds mature don't expect the amount received to be equal to the face value. This investment product works to your best advantage when the bonds are purchased and then forgotten about until they mature.

| Certificates of deposit (CDs) | Debt instruments issued by banks. | CDs mature anywhere from a few weeks to a few years. | Getting your hands on the money invested into CDs before they mature means paying a penalty—one that could affect the principal amount invested. Because getting this cash back before its time comes with a fee, it's best to follow the rules. In other words, when you decide to invest in CDs—you can do so with as little as $100—choose ones that mature within the time frames that work best for you. |
| U.S. Treasury bills, notes, and bonds | Debt securities issued by the U.S. government. | These three products are backed by the full faith and credit of the U.S. government. That means, it's Uncle Sam who will pay you back the principal invested and from whom you'll receive all interest payments due from these investments. | Once issued, U.S. Treasury bills have maturity dates of up to 1 year; U.S. Treasury notes have maturity dates of between 1 and 5 years; and U.S. Treasury bonds have maturity dates of 5 to 30 years. |

Moving Out on the Investment Risk Scale

The distinction between what is considered to be a moderate risk investment and what is considered an aggressive risk investment product is at best blurred. Deciding between the two is a decision only you—and your instincts—can make.

With that in mind, here's a look at some of the most common kinds of investment products people choose when looking for moderate to aggressive risk investments for their long-term retirement plans.

Stocks

The words *stock* and *equity* are interchangeable. Each represents ownership in a corporation.

If you own stock in a company, you're a shareholder in that corporation, which means you are a part owner of it. As such, you'll share in the profits of that company, provided the per-share price of the stock goes up, and you will receive dividends from it, if the corporation decides to pay its shareholders dividends.

There are literally thousands of different stocks to own. The bulk of them are traded on stock exchanges like the New York Stock Exchange, the American Stock Exchange, and the National Association of Securities Dealers Automated Quotations, or NASDAQ.

Along with the variety in numbers of stocks comes a variety in types. Some are blue-chip stocks, stocks from large, well-established companies; growth stocks, those in which the company right along with its stock price are expected to increase in value quicker than blue-chip stocks; value stocks, which usually have current per-share prices that are viewed as low in comparison with the company's real worth; multinational stocks, involving corporations with facilities both inside and outside of the United States; small cap stocks, stocks from companies that aren't as large as the ones mentioned above but have historically performed better than large companies; and international stocks, ones domiciled in other countries like England, Spain, Thailand, Japan, or Canada.

DIVIDEND REINVESTMENT PROGRAMS (DRIPs)

DRIPs are *dividend reinvestment programs.* For the long-term investor these programs offer a great way to accumulate more shares of a company's stock easily and often without the added cost of a brokerage commission. They work like this: When a publicly held company pays its shareholders dividends and then allows those shareholders the opportunity of reinvesting—or spending that dividend money to purchase more shares of the company's stock—that program is referred to as a DRIP.

Although not all publicly held companies pay dividends to their shareholders and not all companies that pay dividends offer DRIPs (you can ask your broker whether or not a company has a dividend reinvestment program), one national organization makes DRIP investing easily accessible.

That organization is the National Association of Investors Corporation (NAIC). Members of NAIC are given an opportunity to buy shares in many of the companies offering DRIPs. There's a one-time fee for joining NAIC, currently that's $32, and a one-time $5 charge to set up your account with the company offering the DRIP. Each different company you choose to invest in requires that five-dollar fee.

After the initial fees are paid, you can open an account with as little money as it takes to buy one share of that company's stock. NAIC then offers investors who don't have piles of disposable income on hand an affordable way to become shareholders in some of America's largest corporations.

If you'd like to learn more about NAIC, here's their address and telephone number:

NAIC
1515 East Eleven Mile Road
Royal Oak, MI 48067
Telephone: 1-810-583-6242

STOCKS, BONDS, BILLS, AND INFLATION

Ever wonder how the annual returns of some investments compare with the rate of inflation? For the answer to that question, take a look at the following chart.

Type of product	Compound annual return from 1926 through 1994, %
Small-company stocks	12.2
Large-company stocks	10.2
Long-term government bonds	4.8
U.S. Treasury bills	3.7
Inflation	3.1

SOURCE: *Stocks, Bonds, Bills, and Inflation,* Ibbotson Associates, Chicago (annually updated work by Roger G. Ibbotson and Rex A. Singuefield). Used with permission. All rights reserved.

Looking at these figures, it's easy to see why the pros have considered stocks as appropriate long-term investments for those investing for their retirement: Stocks historically have outperformed all other asset classes.

Investing in stocks provides an opportunity for investors to have their money grow at rates that frequently will exceed the rate of inflation. However, the stock market is a two-way street. There are profits and losses made from stock investing every business day of every year. Thinking that stock investing is always a sure bet is setting yourself up for a disaster. Even in spite of all the wonderful charts showing how over the long run stocks make investors money, not all stocks make money for every investor.

With that in mind, stocks, over the long term, have shown themselves to be inflation protectors. (See inset "Stocks, Bonds, Bills, and Inflation.")

Selecting stocks for your retirement accounts or personal portfolio takes some thought and research. Individual investors I know who have made the most money in the stock market are those who invest in companies that they know something about and who are familiar with what those companies do. One example of this type of investor might be someone who works for a publicly traded corporation and knows first hand how the company works, how well it's managed, or what's on tap for future development. Another potentially successful strategy is to purchase stock in companies that produce products that you like and buy. One Florida investor who owns a few hundred shares of the FPL Group (Florida Power and Light) bought that utility stock because he uses FPL's power every day of his life. "What can you do without electricity? Besides, power companies have no sense of humor when it comes to not paying your bill, so I know the company is not going to go broke."

Bonds

Bonds are debt instruments, like IOUs. Corporate, taxable, or tax-free bonds are debt securities issued by corporations, the U.S. government, and municipalities. (They are also considered "conservative" investments by many. But, as we pointed out earlier, they do have risks.)

These debt instruments typically reward their investors by making interest payments to them from the time the bond is purchased until the date it is either sold or matures, whatever comes first. Usually payments are made twice a year, every six months, and the interest payment income from them is either taxable, if you've invested in corporate bonds; tax-free, if you've selected tax-exempt municipal bonds as an investment choice; or exempt from state and local—but not federal—taxes, if you've invested in Treasury securities or Series EE savings bonds.

What are the risks in bond investing? The answer depends upon four things:

1. *Quality.* Who you have lent your money to—that is, who the issuer of the bond is.

2. *Maturity.* How long you've given them the right to use your money—that is, until the bond's maturity date.

3. *Credit.* What the odds are that you'll get your money back—that is, receive timely interest and principal payments.

4. *Market conditions.* Interest rate changes affect the prices on bonds as do supply and demand.

HOW INTEREST RATES AFFECT BOND PRICES

If you're a bond investor who buys and holds bonds until they mature, any changes in interest rates won't affect the income those bonds provide you with each year, or the face value you will receive when they mature. *But* if you don't plan on holding your bonds until they mature, any changes in interest rates will affect the money you receive should you sell your bonds before they mature. (Interest income from those bonds remains constant until you no longer are their holder.)

Table 8-2, from Fidelity Investments, shows the estimated price movement of Treasury bonds with varying maturities, assuming that over the next year interest rates will go up or down one percentage point from current levels. (Since Treasury bonds are backed by the full faith and credit of the U.S. government, it is assumed there is no credit risk affecting bond price movements.) This does not reflect the performance of any Fidelity fund. Fidelity funds are not insured or guaranteed by the U.S. government.

Table 8-2. Estimated Price Movement of Treasury Bonds

Maturity	Yield (%)	If interest rates rise 1%, price would FALL...(%)	If interest rates fall 1%, price would RISE...(%)
■ Short-term bond (2 years in maturity)	5.6	− 1.84	+ 1.89
■ Intermediate-term bond (10 years in maturity)	7.05	− 6.78	+ 7.42
■ Long-term bond (30 years maturity)	7.34	− 10.97	+ 13.36

Those credit, quality, maturity, and market condition points are important. Here's why. In the bond world, the longer the maturity on a bond, the riskier it becomes. That's why bonds maturing in 30 years offer investors higher rates of returns than those maturing in 6 months or 5 years. So, theoretically, the safest bonds are those with the shortest maturities. They are also, however, the ones offering the lowest yields. And, as we pointed out earlier, safe, low-return investments can still be risky because their returns don't always keep up with inflation over the long run.

As far as quality is concerned, many bonds are rated. The highest rating possible on a bond is triple-A; the lowest, "nr" or nonrated. Nonrated bonds typically offer investors higher returns than triple-A-rated ones do. So, if you're looking for the highest yield possible from a bond investment, odds are it's going to be from a nonrated 30-year maturing bond, rather than a triple-A-rated corporate bond with a 2-year maturity. One word of caution: because bond issuers have to pay to obtain a bond rating, a nonrated bond might not be a low-rated bond. It could simply be a bond with no rating.

Three well-known agencies that rate bonds are Standard & Poor's, Moody's Investors Service, and Fitch Investors Services. To find out how a bond is rated, either ask your broker or financial advisor for that information or go to your local library. The library will probably have information in their reference department from one, if not all three, of those rating agencies.

Market conditions affect the prices on bonds, too. And as was already pointed out, when interest rates change, so does the price of a bond. That means, if you own a bond and have to sell it *before* it matures, you may or may not get back the original price that you paid for it.

Zero-Coupon Bonds

Zero-coupon bonds are another investment worth noting. These "stripped-coupon" bonds can be issued by governments, corporations, and municipalities, too, which means they may be taxable or tax-free investments. Stripped-coupon bonds are ones that don't pay interest rates twice a year. Like U.S. savings bonds, zero-coupon bonds are also sold at prices that are discounts of their face values.

Here's an example: A $1000 face value zero-coupon municipal bond might have a 5 percent coupon on it, mature in the year 2010, and cost only $350 to purchase. If you buy that bond and hold it until it matures, you'll get $1000 back. So zero-coupon bonds can fit nicely into someone's long-term retirement plans because they are inexpensive to invest in.

The downside to zero-coupon bonds is that they are usually best utilized as buy-and-hold investments. If you need to sell them before they mature, current interest rates at the time you sell will determine whether you get back more or less than the original amount invested.

Wealth Builder Tip_____

Bonds held until they mature provide investors with an I-know-what-I've-got-kind-of-product.

For example, if someone is the owner of a $10,000 (in face value), triple-A-rated corporate bond with a 6 percent coupon on it maturing in the year 2007, that person can expect that every year that bond will pay her $600—in two payments of $300 each—until the year 2007, when it matures. At that time she will also receive the face value of the bond, too. In this case that would be $10,000.

While there is no disputing the comfort of knowing what an investment will return during its lifetime, returns from bonds don't always keep up with the inflation rate. This means a retirement portfolio made up of only bonds might not have the buying power in the future that it does today.

Mutual Funds

Mutual funds are professionally managed packaged products. Each fund is different and is generally made up of either a variety of stocks, a variety of bonds, or a variety of a little bit of both. Because thousands of investors can buy shares of the same mutual fund, mutual funds are called *pooled* investments. And because mutual funds don't invest into just one security, like one stock or one bond, they are called *diversified* products. Picking and choosing the securities that make up a mutual fund's portfolio is done by either an individual or a team of portfolio managers. (Just as artists have portfolios in which they place their works, inside a mutual fund's portfolio are the different securities and investments that that fund's professional managers have purchased.)

Of the over 5300 different open-end mutual funds around, all share one common goal: Every portfolio manager wants to make money for the fund's investors, its shareholders.

Open-end mutual funds are the ones investors are most familiar with. They are named open-end because shares of them are continually being issued and redeemed. There's no limit to the number of shares that an open-end fund can create. Buying open-end mutual funds can be done through brokers, banks, financial advisors and planners, or directly from the mutual fund companies themselves. Closed-end mutual funds are another kind of investment fund. They differ from open-end funds in that, like the stock of a publicly held company, only a specific number of shares of each fund are issued. Because there is a limit to the number of shares issued, the per-share price on a closed-end mutual fund may be more or less than what the value of all the securities in that fund's portfolio represents.

There is more to buying shares of closed-end funds than meets the eye so make sure to learn as much as possible about this kind of fund before investing. Closed-end funds can only be purchased from a broker.

Investors in mutual funds are called shareholders. The buying and selling of shares of mutual funds can be done any business day of the week, making these products "liquid"—that is, it's easy to sell the shares of an open-end fund and get your money back. How much money you get back after that sale, however, may be more or less than what was originally invested.

Each mutual fund has an investment objective; some invest for income, others for growth, others for both. There also are different types of mutual funds. The Investment Company Institute (ICI), the trade association for mutual funds, classifies mutual funds into roughly two dozen different categories from aggressive growth funds (those that hope to return the maximum growth possible for their shareholders) to money-market mutual funds (short-term investments in which fund assets are placed in securities maturing in a few days or weeks or months and in which fund shares are targeted to be both bought and sold at $1 per share).

Mutual funds can be a convenient way for those of us with only a little money to start building a nest egg for our retirements. There are literally dozens of well-established mutual funds in which $50, $100, or $250 is all that is needed to open an account. Plus there are funds in which small amounts of money—like $50—will start you on a monthly investing plan. There is more about these "investomatic" programs later in this chapter.

The pitfalls of mutual fund investing are the same as those of straight stock or bond investing. There are always risks involved, and none come with a written guarantee of making you a profit.

To learn more about mutual funds, the ICI makes a number of different pamphlets and brochures available to everyone. They are free for the asking. Titles include

"What Is a Mutual Fund? Eight Fundamentals"

"Discipline: It Can't Really Be Good for You, Can It?"

"Money Market Mutual Funds—A Part of Every Financial Plan"

"An Investor's Guide to Reading the Mutual Fund Prospectus"

To obtain these or any other information that the ICI offers on mutual funds, write or fax them at the following:

Investment Company Institute
1401 H Street, NW
Washington, DC 20005-2148
Fax: 202-326-5874

Or pick up a copy of my book *Straight Talk about Mutual Funds* (McGraw-Hill, 1992) at your local bookstore or library. It's an easy-to-read primer about mutual funds.

The next chapter covers mutual fund investing in more detail.

Life Insurance Products

Life insurance products, among other things, offer the long-term investor another way to accumulate monies tax-deferred.

The life insurance products most of us are familiar with are term insurance, whole-life, variable life, and universal life policies.

Term insurance, as the name implies, is an insurance policy created for a specific amount of time such as 10, 20, or 30 years. The big selling point of a term policy is that it offers insurance coverage to a young person at inexpensive premiums. (A "premium" is the insurance industry's name for "payment.") Families just starting out who want to make sure that they will have some money should the breadwinner in that family suddenly die often take out term life policies.

Term life insurance gets more costly as you age, because you become a higher risk for the insurance company. It also does not have any cash value to it like other kinds of insurance policies do. So when the term life policy expires, that's it. It's over. There will be no financial rewards on the day this policy ends. Its rewards come only when a death occurs while a policy is still in force.

Whole-life insurance policies are permanent life insurance policies—ones in which, upon the insureds' deaths, the beneficiaries of the policies receive a payment that's fixed and was created at the onset of the policies. The premiums paid on these policies can be made for life or for a specific amount of time.

Universal life insurance contracts are basically whole-life policies with some added flexibilities. Policyholders here can vary the amount and timing of their premium payments to meet their needs. Death benefits are flexible in these policies and their cash value is based on the premiums paid and market conditions.

Variable and fixed annuities and guaranteed investment contracts (GICs) are also investment vehicles that fall under the insurance umbrella. There's more on each of these investments later in this section.

The world of life insurance—and all the various kinds of investment products it makes available—is an intricate one, with thousands upon thousands of licensed people selling insurance policies. According to one financial expert, there are 250,000 full-time and 150,000 part-time insurance agents out there. Whoa!

Insurance products are for the long-term investor. Short-term investing isn't what insurance is all about. That's because there are costs like commissions, administrative fees, surrender charges, mortality fees, and sometimes even a state premium tax on insurance products that, when added together, can make these products costly should you have to cancel a policy or contract during its first few years of ownership.

Terry Savage, in her book *Terry Savage's New Money Strategies for the '90s* (Harper Business, 1993), says that there are only three reasons to buy life insurance:

1. To replace income if the insured person dies prematurely and family members depend on that income.
2. To provide money to buy out a business partner, repay business loans, or hire a successor in case of an owner's death.
3. To provide immediate, liquid money to pay estate taxes.

How much life insurance people need depends upon their individual life circumstances: their age, their marriage status, whether they have children, whether both spouses are working, and what their income level is. Some rules of thumb as to how much life insurance people should have are:

1. If you're single with no dependents, most pros say you might not need life insurance.

2. One way of gauging how much life insurance you need is to set the total dollar coverage at somewhere between five and eight times your current annual wages.

Annuities

Annuities are among the hottest-selling investment products around. One of the reasons long-term investors like these investments—which are contracts with insurance companies—is because the money in them grows tax-deferred.

There are three kinds of annuities to choose from:

1. *Deferred fixed annuities.*   Investments into deferred fixed annuity contracts can be either one-time lump-sum investments or made in periodic payments. These contracts yield a fixed return for a specific amount of time, like a 5 percent return for five years. Yield is quoted at the time the investment is made.

2. *Deferred variable annuities.*   These are basically mutual funds with an insurance wrapper around them. In variable annuity contracts

investors may also either invest one lump sum of money or add to those contracts periodically. Then they may choose from a variety of different funds to invest in. That means the financial risks and the rewards of variable annuity investing are different than those of fixed-rate annuities. So, depending upon the variable annuity investment selected, the performance of the stock and/or bond markets will impact the results on this investment.

3. *Immediate annuities.* In this investment, once a lump sum is deposited, you begin receiving payments from the annuity contracts immediately.

Annuities have some additional appeals too. Unlike IRAs, 401(k)s, or Keoghs, there aren't any limits on the amount of money that can be invested in them.

You also don't have to start taking your money out of annuities at age 70½. Many times monies can stay invested up to age 80 or 85. And these policies usually have a death benefit that guarantees the beneficiary an amount of money that's equal to what was originally invested or the contract value, whichever is greater. Plus assets in them pass directly to the beneficiary, avoiding probate. So they offer some appeal to those people seeking a long-term tax-deferred investment.

GICs

Guaranteed investment contracts (GICs) are insurance company products that provide a fixed rate of return to their investors. But don't be fooled by the name. The "guarantee" in GICs is a promise to make payments that is not backed by the full faith and credit of the U.S. government, like Treasury bonds are. Rather, it's a guarantee to pay that's backed by the insurance company offering the product.

Studies show that GICs have been one of the top investment choices for the 401(k) investor. Critics of the product argue that a fixed rate of return, although constant, is generally no match for inflation. Still others say that a fixed positive rate of return is better than no rate of return at all—and much better than a negative return.

Consider a GIC investment product as you would any other fixed-income conservative investment—remembering that they are designed for income, not growth of principal.

Some Pros and Cons of Insurance Products

Insurance products may or may not fit into your long-term retirement plan. When evaluating them, keep in mind that insurance is basically another type of long-term investment vehicle. As such, it may not be appropriate for your own personal long-term needs or it could complement your long-term plans very nicely.

When I told a fellow writer that I was going to include insurance products in this book, she said, "Don't forget the 'God forbid'."

I had to laugh because I don't think that there's an insurance agent in the country who hasn't included in his sales pitch a "God forbid" clause. One that goes something like this: "God forbid your husband should die young, Mrs. Jones, but we all saw what happened to Mr. Henry, didn't we? Left his wife penniless...."

So on behalf of my writer friend, don't be seduced into buying a life insurance policy because of a sales pitch.

Here are five things to ask about when first looking into insurance policies:

1. *Ask about the company's rating.* Insurance companies have ratings. The highest rating possible is an A+. A. M. Best is one of the best known firms for rating insurance companies. Others who rate insurance companies include Standard & Poor's, Moody's, Duff & Phelps, and Weiss Research. Ratings on insurance companies can, and do, change. So use a rating as *one* piece of information from which to evaluate a product, not as the *only* piece.

2. *Check out how long the insurance company has been around.* Use the sources mentioned above, available in your library's research department, to find that information out.

3. *Ask about guarantees, surrender charges, and cash values of the policies you're interested in.* Make sure to understand what each is and how each can affect you.

4. *Work with a reputable insurance agent.* Insurance sales agents must be licensed. After they've received that licensing, they may work independently or for insurance agencies; some may be chartered financial consultants or certified financial planners and members of the American Society of CLUs (chartered life underwriters). Many stockbrokers even have insurance licenses. To find a good agent ask those whose opinions you respect the most who their insurance agents are and interview a few of them before selecting the one who you think is the best qualified and with whom you would like to work. Finding a good insurance agent is important. You are, afterall, likely to do business with this individual throughout your entire life.

5. *Ask yourself why you are buying the policy and what needs it is meeting.* Then make sure the policy you have selected really meets those needs.

Alan Lavine, author of *Your Life Insurance Options* (Wiley, 1993), offers these general observations about life insurance products:

- You buy life insurance for income protection.

- Term insurance is only low-cost protection when you are young. It gets more expensive as you get older.

- Whole-life insurance is permanent protection. Part of your premium is used to buy insurance, part goes into an interest-bearing savings account.

- If you buy a universal life insurance policy, you can determine how much must be paid in premium every year.

- With a variable life insurance policy, your cash value can be invested in common stock and bond mutual funds.

- After you buy the policy, you have 10 days to look it over. If you don't like the policy, the insurance company will refund your money.

- You can borrow against the cash value in your insurance policy at low rates and without a credit check.

- You don't pay state or federal income tax on the cash value buildup in your insurance policy.

To learn more about these investment products, here are some easy-to-read sources:

Information from the Investment Company Institute.

Alan Lavine, *Your Life Insurance Options*, New York: John Wiley, 1993.

Terry Savage, *Terry Savage's New Money Strategies for the '90s*, New York: HarperCollins, 1993.

Dian Vujovich, *Straight Talk about Mutual Funds*, New York: McGraw-Hill, 1992.

Analyzing a Product in Terms of Its Risks

Table 8-3 gives a general overview of some of the different kinds of investment products vis-à-vis the risks involved, the inflation protection, and the return potential of each.

Table 8-3. Overview of Different Kinds of Investments

Investment	Inflation protection	Return potential
Savings accounts	Low	Low
U.S. savings bonds	Low	Low
Certificates of deposit (CDs)	Low	Low
Money-market funds	Low	Low
U.S. Treasury bills	Low	Low
U.S. government bonds	Moderate	Moderate
Corporate bonds:		
Investment-grade	Moderate	Moderate
Low-rated	Moderate	High
Common stocks:		
Large company	High	High
Small company	High	High

Compared to What? Gauging Investment Returns

Once you've become a believer in investing for your retirement, having something to compare your investment returns with is vitally important.

Indices like the Dow Jones Industrial Average (DJIA) or the Standard & Poor's 500 (S&P 500) provide investors with two different ways of gauging the performance of stocks and stock mutual funds.

Here's a brief overview of some popular market indices and which ones to use depending upon the kind of stock, bond, or mutual fund investments you've made:

- If you're investing primarily in the stocks of large-capitalization U.S. domestic companies, or mutual funds that make this kind of investment, use the DJIA or S&P 500 and Russell 3000 to gauge the performance of these investments.

- If your style is to invest in small-cap U.S. stocks, or small-cap U.S. stock funds, check the performances of the NASDAQ Composite Index, the Russell 2000 index, and the Wilshire 4500 index.

- For those investing in international stock and international stock funds (funds that invest the bulk of their assets in companies located outside of the United States), use the Morgan Stanley EAFE Index (EAFE stands for Europe, Australia, and Far East) for the best comparisons.

- If you're a global stock fund fan (global funds can invest both within the United States and abroad), check the EAFE Index along with the appropriate U.S. indices.

- For individual bond investors as well as bond fund shareholders, both Lehman Brothers and Salomon Brothers have bond indices for all ranges of the domestic as well as foreign bond markets. Two popular indices for funds investing in the United States would be the Lehman Government/Corporate Bond Index or the Salomon Brothers Broad Investment Grade Bond Index.

You'll find indices like the DJIA, the S&P 500, and NASDAQ listed in the business section of your newspaper. If they aren't there, pick up a copy of *The Wall Street Journal* and/or one of the weekly publications of *Barron's* for a complete overview of the market indices.

Can Investment Risk Be Measured?

There's no two ways about it, living life involves taking risks. On any given day or night the list of risks we take is endless.

You could slip and fall on a slippery floor in the kitchen or bathroom at any time of the day or night. Or you could be confronted with a zillion and one unforeseen happenstances while leaving the house, going off to work, driving a car, or riding in a train, plane, or boat. Then there are the risks involved in loving someone—or in leaving them. Not to mention the risks we take in the workplace or on vacation.

But there are differences between the risks we take in our personal lives and the ones we take when investing our dollars. Those differences boil down to measurability: Some risks are more measurable than others.

The risk a pedestrian takes when walking across the street isn't usually considered a measurable risk—particularly when that person crosses a street at the corner and waits for the streetlight to turn green before crossing. But the risk involved when buying 100 shares of Southern Bell is something different. It's a measurable one.

When it comes to investing, taking measurable risks means doing some research to get a sense of how big, or how small, a risk you are taking with your money before you ever invest it.

Taking the time to do some research, like looking at the performance of an investment, seeing how it has changed over time, and comparing

it to others in like categories, is one way to begin measuring—or calculating—the kinds of money risks you could be taking.

But even after all the research is completed, investing still will
never be 100 percent risk-free. Three of the common risks involved
with investing are market risk, purchasing power risk, and out-of-the-
blue risk.

Market Risk

Whether you're investing in stocks, bonds, mutual funds, oil paintings, or PEZ dispensers, the price on each continues to change within
the markets where each is traded.

For instance, 40 years ago Christie's may have auctioned off a Degas
painting now and then, but a PEZ dispenser? Hardly. Who would have
ever guessed that those long little plastic candy boxes with the goofy
caricature heads would be collectors' items in the 1990s? But they are.

How long the PEZ collectible trend will continue on is anybody's
guess. It's also where the market risk for this collectible begins: Will
the price paid for something—like a PEZ dispenser, or shares of a
stock or mutual fund or a bond—be higher tomorrow than it is today?
Or will it be lower? The answer to that question is something nobody
knows for sure—until tomorrow has come and the investment is to be
sold.

Purchasing Power Risk

Inflation, as we've pointed out before, has become a real part of our
American economic fabric. During the early 1990s it averaged about 3
percent a year. That means that prices on goods and services are
increasing about 3 percent a year. At that rate, a cup of coffee and a
donut that you can buy for a buck today could essentially cost $1.03
next year. At a 3 percent inflation rate, the prices of goods and services
double every 24 years.

Historically, however, the rate of inflation has bounced all around.
In the early '40s, '50s, and the mid-'70s and early '80s the inflation rate
was up over 10 percent. At a 10 percent rate of inflation, prices double
every seven years!

When the rate of inflation falls, or deflates, prices go down. So along
with inflation there have also been times in this century when prices
deflated or even remained stagnant.

Therefore, purchasing power risk in the investment arena has to do
with future prices and how much your money will buy. Here's an
example of how future purchasing power works hand in hand with
the investment choices that you make.

If, over the next 30 years, you are a conservative investor, choosing only to invest in CDs or GICs and a simple savings account, and the average annual return on all of those investments combined is 4 percent, if the rate of inflation over that same time period averages 6 percent, your nest egg won't be able to buy tomorrow what it can today. So, even though you may create a dandy-sized nest egg, you will lose some purchasing power because the rate of inflation over the 30-year period will be higher than the return your investments bring in.

If, however, your investments average a rate of return of 8 percent, this invested money will be working for you at a rate that beats inflation (in our example) and gives you more money to spend—or greater purchasing power than the rate of inflation!

Inflation is one of the reasons financial experts suggest investing in growth securities such as stocks or stock mutual funds.

So beware and be aware of inflation. This mysterious demon can sneak in and reduce the value of money without us ever seeing it. Inflation can be elusive as well as destructive. It is the reason why we can't just save our money in piggy banks or cookie jars until we have a pile big enough to live on forever. To beat inflation means taking some risks with our hard-earned cash. These risks may seem frightening, but if taken in small doses, they can prove to be very rewarding.

Out-of-the-Blue Changes

It's impossible to predict, or in many cases, even think up all the different circumstances that could effect the future value of an investment you've made.

Let's say, for example, that you're a big fan of real estate. Buying raw land to you makes good sense and you believe it can offer wonderful financial rewards, particularly if you "buy right" and in a desirable location. After all, as a spokesperson on one TV commercial says, "Land. They don't make it anymore."

So in an effort to create a comfy nest egg, you decide to purchase a few acres of prime waterfront property along the mighty Mississippi River. And it's beautiful property. So beautiful that you decide to add to the value of that land by building a home on it. Then you decide to live in that home for a while before selling it at what you hope will be a whopping profit.

All is well for these dream plans until floods like the ones of 1993 come rolling along. Before you know it, that beautiful riverfront property, and the home on it, winds up, not as riverfront, but underwater property. Ouch! Thanks to Mother Nature, your land investment doesn't increase in value, it gets stuck in the mud.

Nature isn't the only one that can play a trick on our investment dreams. Changes in tax laws can make what once was a good investment opportunity lose its luster. Or product developments can make a good idea turn obsolete. Remember IBM's mainframe computers? Originally they were huge and took temperature-controlled rooms to contain. Today the computer world is hundreds of times bigger than it used to be 20 years ago while computers themselves are hundreds of times smaller.

Again, there are no 100 percent totally guaranteed for-sure gains to be made in the investment arena. If someone is telling you so, they probably aren't telling you the whole truth.

But there are money-making opportunities—thousands upon thousands of them, all of which require taking some degree of risks. So, while investing comes with its risks, it also comes with its rewards, too. If you do your homework and look into the background and performance history of the investments you'd like to make, the risks that those investments involve are likely to surface. With that information you'll then be able to make some educated measurable-risk decisions about whether or not to invest.

Here are some publications that will help you research stocks, bonds, and mutual funds:

Standard & Poor's Stock Guide.   Published monthly, ask your broker for a free copy or check the reference section at your local library for it.

Standard & Poor's Bond Guide.   Published monthly, check the reference section at your local library for it.

Value Line.   Look for Value Line publications for stock and mutual fund data. This data is generally available in the reference section of your library or by subscription.

Morningstar.   Check the reference section at your local library for Morningstar data on mutual funds, variable annuities, and closed-end funds.

CDA Wiesenberger Investment Company Services.   Another resource for mutual funds; also found at most libraries.

Lipper Analytical Services.   This mutual fund research company is responsible for many of the fund rankings seen in places like *The Wall Street Journal* and other newspaper and magazine publications. Look for their research in the reference section of your library.

The Thomas J. Herzfeld Encyclopedia of Closed-End Funds.   A resource of data on closed-end mutual funds. Also probably found in your local library's reference section.

9
Investing in Mutual Funds

It's the Long Term, Baby

I met Ben on a flight from Dallas to San Antonio last fall. Once I told him I was a mutual fund columnist and author of a book on the subject, he began telling me how mutual funds had proved to be a fabulous investment product for him and his family.

"You know," said this father of two, "In all the years my wife and I have been married, we've never had to worry about money. And it's all because I made some good investments in mutual funds and kept on investing in them throughout the years."

Ben hit the fund jackpot by initially investing a lump sum of money—$5000 to be exact—into an equity fund in 1979. And, as time went on, he contributed $100 a month to that investment. When I met him, he'd been making monthly contributions into that one stock fund for about 14 years.

"It's really been fun to see that money grow," he said. "When it grew in value from four to five figures that was one thing. But when it got to six figures, my wife and I could hardly believe it."

There's a lot to be learned from Ben's investment success story—especially after you get over your pangs of jealousy and envy for this guy and the "Why didn't I do that?" guilt trip accompanying those feelings. But, the fact is, you *can* do that.

The biggest investment learning lesson that Ben's experience can teach us is: long-term investing in stock funds can pay off—big. (See inset, "Does Mutual Fund Investing Really Pay Off?") In fact, according to Ibbotson, a Chicago-based research company, between 1926 and the close of 1994, the compound annual return for investments in small-company growth stocks has averaged about 12.2 percent a year; those in blue-chip stocks, about 10.2 percent annually.

Investing for that same period of time in Treasury bills and bonds hasn't been as profitable. The compound annual return on those investments has averaged 3.7 and 4.8 percent, respectively.

DOES MUTUAL FUND INVESTING REALLY PAY OFF?

It does according to the chart on page 105, which is a look at how $1 would have grown in value if invested in different kinds of mutual funds if that investment began on December 31, 1975, and ended on December 31, 1994.

The numbers in the chart assume that all dividends and capital gains have been reinvested back into the funds, no taxes have been paid, and performance reflects the compound annual return for the various fund types.

Investment Strategies

One retirement investment strategy is to invest only in mutual funds, using them in both your qualified retirement accounts—like in 401(k)s, IRAs, Keoghs, or SEP-IRAs—as well as in your personal investing portfolio. If this idea appeals to you, there is certainly no shortage of funds to choose from, therefore making it easy to find a fund to meet your investment needs or personal risk levels.

What's important to remember about using only mutual funds is to diversify among them—just as you would if you were creating a portfolio made up of individual stocks and bonds.

Even though a mutual fund by itself invests in a variety of different securities, which makes it a diversified product, loading up on the same types of mutual funds is no way to create a diversified portfolio of mutual fund investments.

Creating a diversified portfolio of mutual funds means investing in various types of funds among various asset classes. So, a diversified portfolio of mutual funds might include

Money-market mutual funds. Depending upon your needs and tax brackets, the interest income from money-market mutual funds may be either taxable or tax-free. Money-market mutual funds invest in securities maturing within a few days to a few weeks. The per-share

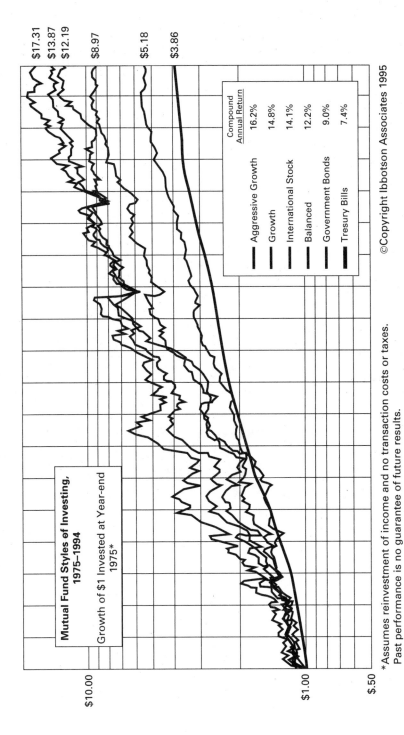

Mutual Fund Styles of Investing, 1975–1994

Growth of $1 Invested at Year-end 1975*

	Compound Annual Return
Aggressive Growth	16.2%
Growth	14.8%
International Stock	14.1%
Balanced	12.2%
Government Bonds	9.0%
Tresury Bills	7.4%

$17.31
$13.87
$12.19
$8.97
$5.18
$3.86

$10.00
$1.00
$.50

©Copyright Ibbotson Associates 1995

*Assumes reinvestment of income and no transaction costs or taxes.
Past performance is no guarantee of future results.

[SOURCE: *Stocks, Bonds, Bills, and Inflation, 1995 Yearbook*, Ibbotson Associates, Chicago (annually updated by Roger Ibbotson and Rex A. Singuefield). Used with permission. All rights reserved.]

price to buy and sell them is usually $1. These funds often make good short-term money parking spots and the interest earned in them is usually more than that earned in bank savings accounts.

Growth funds. These funds are targeted for capital appreciation—that is, hopefully their per-share price will increase. Here, depending upon your risk tolerance level, you might choose a blue-chip growth fund, an aggressive growth fund, international, global funds, or small-company growth funds.

Balanced fund and/or growth and income funds. These funds ideally provide their shareholders with both growth and income opportunities. Income here is received through the dividends that the stocks in these portfolios pay or via the interest income that the bonds in these portfolios kick off.

Bond funds. Choices here range from the short-term corporate, tax-exempt municipal or government funds (short-term funds in which the portfolio managers invest their fund's assets into bonds that have maturity dates of under 2 or 3 years); to medium-term bond funds (investing in bonds that have maturity dates over 5 and under 10 years); to long-term bond funds (those in which the bonds in a fund's portfolios have maturity dates typically beginning in 10 years and ranging out as far as 30 years). Choices regarding the quality of bond funds you can invest in range from triple-A to non-rated.

Specialty and/or sector funds. This grouping would include funds that invest in things like gold and precious metals, or ones that invest in specific areas like utilities or single-country funds.

Retirement Investing Tip: Investment Objectives_____

All mutual funds have investment objectives, that is, the reasoning behind how the funds are invested. Some funds invest only for income, others for capital appreciation, and others for a combination of the two. Make sure to match up a fund's investment objective with your own personal one.

Finding the Right Fund

Choosing a fund to meet your investment needs is the 64-million-dollar question. While there is no one-size-fits-all answer to it, one way to begin that selection process is to focus in on your own investment time horizon. How much time you plan on keeping your money invested narrows down the choices of fund types significantly. An accepted rule of thumb here is, the longer amount of time you have to invest, the more aggressively you can invest your money.

Wealth Builder Tip_____

The money pros say that taking some investment risks can make good sense.

By investing a portion of your money into mutual funds considered riskier than others—like aggressive growth, international, single-country, emerging markets, gold, or junk bond funds—you may add some performance pizzazz to your overall portfolio of mutual funds which might create a bigger nest egg for yourself than you'd planned for.

A Little Bit of Money *Can* Go a Long Way ...

One of the best-kept secrets in the mutual fund industry is the "invest-o-matic"—a monthly investment plan that in time can turn a little bit of money into big piles of it. Such a plan is commonly called an "automatic investment plan," because to participate in it requires opening an account with your favorite mutual fund and then having a set dollar amount transferred on a specific date each month from your bank checking account into that mutual fund account. Invest-o-matic programs are available through nearly all mutual fund families.

According to A. Michael Lipper, president of the mutual fund research firm bearing his name, many mutual fund families offer these monthly investment programs but "not many people take advantage of them."

What's great about an invest-o-matic is that you usually don't need a lot of money to begin participating in it. Often fifty bucks will do.

The Janus Group of Mutual Funds, for instance, is one no-load fund family that aggressively has encouraged people to participate in their automatic investment plan program, formally called The No Minimum Initial Investment Program. (It is named that because it doesn't cost anything to open the account but minimum monthly investments are $50.)

Although Janus won't say what percentage of their shareholder base participates in the program, Chrissy Snyder, vice president of public relations for that firm, says that since they began promoting this program in 1989 there have been very few dropouts and more and more sign-ups.

Snyder said that Janus gets lots of positive feedback from their shareholders participating in this invest-o-matic monthly program. "People write in to thank us for starting that program. ... Some say that the program forced them to save and forced them to dollar cost average." (Dollar cost averaging is an investment strategy that requires investing the same amount of money on a disciplined regular basis.)

The Pioneer Funds is a load fund family that for years has also encouraged people to invest in this easy fashion. The monthly minimum for their automatic investment plan is also a modest $50 per fund account.

Pioneer says that about 11 percent of their individual shareholder accounts (not including retirement accounts) participate in their monthly investment program. This figure is many times higher than what most industry experts guesstimate the average fund complex has in these types of accounts.

According to Anne Patenaude, vice president of marketing at Pioneer, along with the monthly investment program that any individual can open, Pioneer also has a payroll deduction plan that's available to all companies, large and small. Just like the individual plan, all it takes is a commitment of $50 per month—some paperwork for your employer to fill out—and the money is then deducted from your payroll and automatically invested into one of the Pioneer funds.

Participating in an automatic investment program—one that's separate from your employer's payroll deduction plan—requires an electronic transfer of funds from your bank account directly into your mutual fund account. To do that means providing the fund family with your bank account number. If you're a little bit queasy about sharing your bank account number with anyone for fear that more money could be debited from that account than you had originally planned for, make sure to read the agreement the fund supplies before setting up these preauthorized withdrawals. Then ask your bank for information about Regulation E, Electronic Fund Transfers, a Federal Reserve Board rule outlining the rights and rules for the preauthorized transfer of funds.

Like most investing programs, the first step—opening the account— is the most difficult one to take. Don't let that one stop you from this very painless way to invest.

As the Markets Fluctuate ...

Nobody likes losing money. And, as the markets showed everyone once again in 1994, not all investments make money every year.

Pennies, dimes, quarters, and dollars can get shaved off stocks, bonds, and mutual fund prices and take the pizzazz out of investing. But not to worry. There are plenty of opportunities for investors in changing market environments. For those who like individual stocks, down markets can provide some investors with buying opportunities. For others it's a time to sell and sit on the sidelines for a while.

Bond investors who don't plan on holding these securities until they mature may find opportunity or disappointment when interest rates change: they may or may not get back what they originally paid for their bonds in changing interest rate environments should they decide to sell these securities.

"What's wonderful about the mutual fund business is that there are many ways to insulate yourself from the downside of the market," says Jonathan Pond, president of Financial Planning Information in Watertown, Massachusetts.

Pond said that part of how investors weather a downturn in the markets depends upon how they think.

"Nothing in your financial life is either/or. And the mindset that some people are going through when markets head downward is often: Either I sell out of my stock funds and go into cash, or, I sit back and tighten my cinch. Or, I get out of my long bond funds because they are dropping in value and get into cash, or, I stick with them."

Pond's suggestions for investors who are stuck in the either/or mindset is this: For bond fund investors, switching from funds in which the portfolios are invested in long-maturing bonds (long bonds would be those maturing in 15, 20, or 30 years) into short or intermediate bond funds makes sense.

Says Pond: "If they go intermediate, they are going to get probably 75 to 80 percent of the yield of a 30-year Treasury or its equivalent with a lot less risk."

For stock fund investors unable to sleep at night because they're worrying about their fund's performance, Pond likes equity income funds rather than the high-risk or volatile sector funds. "These kinds of funds [equity income] will not eliminate the risk of loss but can insulate you in a way that no pure aggressive growth or small-cap fund can."

A. Michael Lipper, president of the mutual fund research company bearing his name, suggests dollar cost averaging for the long-term investor. He said that changing markets is something investors have to accept. And that part of accepting that is "being able to buy through the decline in your fund's per-share price" as investors do when they dollar cost average.

One investment strategy Lipper suggests that investors can use to safeguard their fixed-income portfolio in a changing interest rate environment is laddering: "I've been an advocate of the laddered approach. Even though one's income may change, it does safeguard principal." (A laddered portfolio of bond funds would be one in which a variety of different bond funds were included. Each individual bond fund would have portfolios made up of bonds maturing specifically in either the short, intermediate, or long term.)

For those unable to handle downturns in the markets, like those in 1994, Lipper said that money-market funds make sense. "Even though their yields are low, investors won't lose money there."

In the final analysis, however, Lipper thinks that stocks still make good sense. "For those with strong stomachs," says Lipper, "the current stock prices will look like substantial values at the turn of the century. So I wouldn't be shaken out of these positions once I understood that these things can go down."

Mutual Funds and Timing the Market

Diane Ballotti is a broker at Long Grove Trading in Itasca, Illinois. She's lived through both bear and bull markets, selling mutual funds all along the way. One of the things she's learned first-hand is that people don't like to lose money.

"As long as things are going up, people are happy," says Ballotti, a veteran broker for 20 years. "But when things start to go down, they get concerned."

So, in an effort to keep her clients' investment concerns to a minimum, Ballotti has found a market timing program she feels comfortable with.

"We do things differently," says David Moenning, president of Heritage Capital Management, the market timer that Ballotti is a fan of. "Most market timers treat all mutual funds the same. ... They use a model made up of market components and when that model goes positive, they move all their clients. It doesn't matter what type of fund they are in. ... And that's kind of silly because a small-cap aggressive growth fund won't act anything like a big blue-chip stock fund."

Working off the premise that not all funds react alike to changing market conditions, Moenning's market timing plan is a commonsense one that zeros in and follows individual funds. To date, he's got a market timing plan for over twenty different mutual funds.

While it's difficult to dispute the rationale behind a marketing timing plan using specific funds, there are some basics every fund investor needs to understand before seeking out a market timing program. For openers, if you are truly a long-term investor—one who can and will leave their investments alone to weather the storms of all market conditions for say 10, 15, or 20 years—market timing isn't necessary. But Moenning says that most people can't sit through a 10 percent decline in the value of their portfolio. If they can, "more power to them and they definitely don't need me."

Second, market timing isn't designed to enhance a fund's performance in bull markets; its purpose is to lighten the per-share price fall and preserve capital in down, or bear, markets. That's accomplished by selling shares—then buying them back—after they've had a shift in price. Common sell signals for market timers aren't after a hefty drop in share price but typically after minimal changes such as 4, 5, or 7 percent change in per-share price.

For example, here's a comparison of how the overall long-term performance of Twentieth Century's Growth Fund, a stock fund, would fare using three different investment strategies: a buy-and-hold investment philosophy; selling when the fund shares dropped 20 percent from their original price, buying back when they gained 20 percent; and selling when the fund share prices dropped after a 5 percent decline in price, buying back again when those shares increased in price 5 percent. (This example was prepared by Twentieth Century, independent of Moenning's program.)

The value of a $10,000 investment in the Twentieth Century Growth Fund made on January 1, 1973, and ending December 31, 1993, using a buy-and-hold strategy, excluding taxes and with reinvestment of all dividends and interest, would have been $372,879; a timing strategy based on a 20 percent change in price would have yielded $97,902; and one based around a 5 percent price change, $335,704.

As you can see, the worst-performing investment strategy was the one in which you waited for a 20 percent decline in the market to make any timing changes, and the best result came with a buy-and-hold strategy. Much better performance numbers than the 20 percent example happened when you bought and sold fund shares when their net asset value moved 5 percent in one direction or another.

But there are the costs involved here. Some of these include annual timing fees that run approximately 2 percent of assets, if you're using a timer like Moenning. Plus there could be a sales charge from the fund along with additional fees for switching in, out, and among funds within a fund family.

Then, don't forget the taxes. Every time you buy or sell fund shares some kind of taxable event has been created—unless your fund is in a tax-deferred account.

All of which means that there is much more to timing the market than simply buying and selling fund shares when their prices move a few percentage points.

Lump-Sum Investing versus Dollar Cost Averaging

When it comes to making money, which is the better investment approach for mutual fund investors: lump-sum investing or dollar cost averaging?

Lump-sum investing in mutual funds literally means making a one-time investment into a fund. You might do this, say, if you were first opening an account and investing $2000 or $3000 into it. Or you might do it when changing jobs and rolling over a lump sum of money from one qualified retirement account into another.

Dollar cost averaging, on the other hand, is an investment strategy that requires less money but takes more discipline. To dollar cost average into any mutual fund all you have to do is to invest the same amount of money, say $50, $100, or $200, at regular intervals, like every month, into the same fund faithfully and then continue to do so no matter what. That means you continue to invest if the share price of your fund were to fall—or if it were to rise.

While dollar cost averaging will lower the average cost per share of your investment over time (that happens because you're consistently investing the same amount of money), the answer as to which is more profitable—lump-sum investing or dollar cost averaging—depends upon what the market conditions are during the lifetime of your investment.

"A lot of people promote dollar cost averaging—over making an initial lump-sum investment—implying that it should improve your return," says Steven Norwitz, vice president of T. Rowe Price Investment Services. "But it does not necessarily improve your return. ..."

Norwitz explained that the advantages to dollar cost averaging are that it brings a disciplined approach to investing, it gets people putting an amount of money that they can afford into an investment, and it takes the emotion out of investing. "It's like buying on the installment plan."

On the other hand, Douglas Fabian, a market timer and editor of *The Fabian Report*, is no fan of this investment strategy. He thinks investors are too emotional and consequently aren't able to dollar cost average effectively for any length of time. So they wind up losers—selling at market bottoms—rather than investment winners.

In a *Fabian Report* titled "How to Avoid Bear Markets," Fabian said that dollar cost averaging "doesn't work" and that it's "highly impractical during bear markets."

Here are two mathematical examples of how lump-sum investing and dollar cost averaging have worked in the past. If you were to compare a $10,000 lump-sum investment in the S&P 500 with a $100-a-month dollar cost averaging approach in the same investment vehicle during the five-year bear market of 1973 through 1977, assuming no taxes were paid and all dividend and income reinvested, the total return of the dollar cost averaging approach would have paid off better than the lump-sum investing. The total return from dollar cost averaging over that time frame was 13.3 percent while the lump-sum investment lost value, −1 percent in total return. But those same investments made during the five-year bull market of 1988 through 1992 had opposite results. Lump-sum investing was the more profitable. It would have resulted in a total return of 109 percent versus the 43.3 percent from dollar cost averaging.

10
A Checklist of Investment Questions

Now that you've become familiar with some of the popular kinds of investing vehicles and investment strategies, there's more to making money than just placing a phone call to your broker or financial advisor. Each investment has its own set of characteristics and quirks. For example, not all bonds are alike; some stocks pay dividends, others don't; and mutual funds can invest their assets in all sorts of different places.

To help you become a savvy long-term investor, below is a checklist of things to investigate when you're thinking about investing in bonds, stocks, mutual funds, or just about anything else. And, at the end of the chapter are two general tips that you can use to your advantage, no matter what kind of investment you are considering.

A Checklist for Bonds

1. Find out who issued the bond and what the money invested in it is to be used for. Do that by asking the name of the bond's issuer and how or where the money collected from the sale of the bonds will be spent.

2. Ask if the bond is a corporate, municipal, or government bond and if the income from it will be taxable or tax-free. Typically the income from corporate and government bonds is taxable while that of municipal bonds is tax-free. There are exceptions here, so make sure

to ask about the tax consequences of the bond before you become a bondholder.

3. Find out if the bond is rated and then what that rating is. Often the issuers of a bond will have that bond rated. (As was pointed out earlier, there is a cost to obtain a bond rating that the issuer must pay, which is one reason why not all bonds have ratings.) Ratings on bonds range from the highest rating of triple-A to the lowest of nonrated.

4. Ask what the bond's maturity date is. Bonds have maturity dates— a time in the future when the principal, or face amount on the bond, comes due and then gets paid to the bondholder.

5. Find out if the bond has a call date and ask what that date is. A call date is the first date at which the issuer may redeem the bond before its scheduled maturity date. Knowing a bond's call date is as important as knowing its maturity date.

6. Ask what the price of the bond is and what its face value is. The face value of a bond is the amount of money that bond is worth when it matures. Bonds can be sold at prices less than the face value amount, in which case they are said to be selling at a "discount"; prices equal to the face value, or at "par"; or at prices higher than their face values, or at a "premium."

7. Check to see how the bond's price and its yield (that is, the interest rate it pays) compare with other bonds of similar quality and maturity.

8. Finally, take your own reality check. Ask yourself why you are investing in bonds, what you like and dislike about these investments, and how long you plan on holding on to the bonds you're purchasing. Buying bonds and holding on to them until they mature is one thing; buying and then trading them is quite another. Because the price of a bond changes as interest rates change, having your ducks in a row as to both why you're investing in bonds and the length of time you plan on holding these investment products is important.

A Checklist for Stocks

1. Find out what the exact name of the corporation you'd like to invest in is, the stock's trading symbol, and the stock exchange(s) that it trades on.

2. Check out the stock's ranking. The Standard & Poor's stock guide ranks stocks. Their highest ranking is A+, the lowest D.

3. Is the stock you are buying common stock or preferred stock?

4. Find out what the company does. Because some corporations produce only one product while others are conglomerates, inquire into all the aspects of the company. Then use that information to do some deductive reasoning and decide for yourself if you like that company's line of business and think it's worth investing your money in.

5. Find out how actively the stock is traded. A stock that doesn't trade often may be difficult to sell.

6. Find out if the stock pays a dividend; how much that dividend is; whether the amount of dividends paid has gone up or down over time; and how long the company has been paying dividends. Companies don't have to pay dividends on their shares of common stock. And even when they do, there is nothing carved in granite that says they have to keep paying those dividends. Finding out a company's past dividend record is particularly important for those planning on receiving income from that investment.

7. Check to see if the company offers a dividend reinvestment plan. DRIPs, or dividend reinvestment plans, allow shareholders to purchase more shares of a company's stock as dividends accrue and without a sales commission. These programs are great ways to build a nest egg effortlessly.

8. Ask yourself precisely why you are buying this stock and how long you plan on owning this security.

A Checklist for Mutual Funds

1. Find out the exact name of the mutual fund you're interested in purchasing shares of and the family from which it comes. There are now well over 5000 different open-end mutual funds to invest in and literally hundreds of different mutual fund families those funds can be a part of, so it's easy to become confused if you are new to the mutual fund investing arena.

2. Ask what the fund's investment objective is and see if that objective matches yours. Mutual funds invest their shareholders' money with a specific investment objective in mind. A fund that invests in Treasury bonds might have as an investment objective safety of principal and income, while one that invests in emerging markets might have as its investment objective capital appreciation. From those two examples you can see how important matching your investment objectives with that of a fund's objectives is.

3. Find out where the fund invests its money. That means asking questions about where the fund invests its assets—for instance, only in U.S. securities or does it invest globally? Then find out what kinds of securities and investment strategies it utilizes—does it invest in options, derivatives, futures? Or common stocks and domestic bonds only?

4. Is there a sales charge on the fund you're interested in buying shares of? If so, what kind of sales charge is it and how much is that charge? (A sales charge is like a commission, part of which gets paid to the individual for selling the product.) Sales charges on mutual funds come in any variety of styles from "load" to "no-load," or "low-load" to "front-load" to "back-end load." Most refer to the time at which the sales charge is to be paid.

5. All mutual funds have annual fees and expenses that shareholders pay each and every year that they own shares of the fund. Make sure to ask how much these fees are. While shareholders won't get a bill directly for these fees each year, they will affect the fund's performance.

6. Check to see how long the mutual fund has been in existence, who the fund manager currently is, and how long he or she has been managing the mutual fund. Some funds are managed by teams, others by computer-driven models. Some funds are new to the marketplace, while others have been around for decades.

7. Make sure to request a prospectus for the fund you're interested in from the fund family before investing. Then *read* that prospectus from front to back. Even if a mutual fund's prospectus may be dull reading, it is chock-full of information that will educate and enlighten you. It's a must read. If you don't understand the words or concepts used in one, ask your broker, financial advisor, or the fund's representative for an explanation.

8. Finally, ask yourself why you're interested in buying shares of a fund, how long you plan on owning shares of the fund, and what kind of performance return you expect to get from this investment. Then make sure to check out that last number with the historic performance averages on the fund itself to see if your expectations are realistic.

A Checklist for Just about Anything

1. Ask yourself what really appeals to you about the investment product. Is it trendy, or a product that makes practical sense and meets your needs.

2. Do you have any experience investing in this area? If not, are you willing to take the time to find out more about this investment other than what the sales brochures or salesperson has told you? If you don't know where to begin learning more about this investment, stop in at your local library. The reference department there has plenty of information about investing and investments, all free for anyone willing to take the time to read.

3. Think about how much this investment is going to cost you to get into and will cost you to maintain. Gold bullion needs safekeeping, as do precious paintings and jewelry and other collectibles. Real estate investments require out-of-pocket expenses and antique cars need a place to be parked. Stocks and bond certificates can be held in vaults or as electronic entries via your brokerage firm. Mutual funds have ongoing annual expenses, and IRAs may have annual fees. Know what these costs and expenses are before becoming an investor.

4. Finally, ask yourself how much money you hope to make from this investment. Once you've got that number in mind, check to see if what you're hoping for is a realistic expectation. Also, compare previous performance results with present prices and look for cycles or trends in the products you're thinking about investing in.

TWO TIPS

When it comes to making investments, there are millions of different places and products to choose from.

If this world of choices seems too big to handle, and you don't know where to begin or which places to invest, here are two helpful tips.

1. Invest in what you know. That means, take advantage of what you've learned in life by using the lessons from your work, home, or recreational environment to provide you with some investment insights.

For instance, if you're a nurse, you probably come in contact with different medical supplies, prescription drugs, and patient needs on a daily basis. Think about the companies that make the products you like, along with the ones who make those you don't care for, and use that information to help you make some investment decisions.

If you're a carpenter, bus driver, heavy machinery driver, seamstress, maintenance or cleaning person, computer whiz, homemaker, or whatever, your profession provides insights into a world that those of us who aren't associated with those jobs know little about. So use your home and work environment to think about what products or companies you might like to invest in.

2. Think about investing your money where you spend it. Each month we spend our money on things like power and telephone calls, food and transportation, and recreational activities and clothing.

Why not sit down and make a list of all the specific places you spend your money? Then decide if you'd like to invest in any of those places. If you pay an NSP (Northern States Power) bill each month, maybe being a shareholder in that company would appeal to you. If you shop at Winn-Dixie, perhaps you'd like to own shares of that grocery chain. What about the car you're driving, the hotels you stay at when you travel, the toys your kids play with, or the products you use to clean your home? All are brought to you by some company; and you could become a shareholder of stock in many of those companies.

Once you begin thinking about investing in the things you know and in the places where your money gets spent, you'll realize that the investment product world is a broad one. You'll also recognize that, as a consumer, each time you buy a product or pay a bill, you're already investing in—or supporting—that particular product or company.

PART 4

Planning for Retirement: A Family Affair

11

Teach Your Children Well

Children and retirement planning might not seem a likely combination, but the truth is that teaching kids about money—how to make it, save it, and grow it—are some of the best lessons any adult, parent, and grandparent can pass on. After all, children learn best by example. You did, and so will your children.

How It Used to Be

When John and Mary Larson started thinking about their retirement, both were in their mid-thirties. And with two children—one in elementary school, the other in junior high—they didn't have the extra cash to do anything but dream about what life would be like when they grew old and gray together.

The picture they painted of their retirement years was one shared by many born around 1920: Work hard for the same company until you are 65. Then sit back and enjoy life thanks to the pension checks you so diligently have earned.

Today the Larson's are in their mid-seventies. And life for them is pretty good. Their primary home in St. Paul, Minnesota, is all paid for; their winter home in Tucson will be paid off in five years; each still is enjoying good health; and their biggest complaint is that their certificates of deposit (CDs) aren't paying the high interest rates they were 10 years ago. Consequently, they have had to tighten their monthly budget more than either had ever expected.

"That means eating at home a little more often than I'd like to," says Mary.

The Larson's children, now both adults and in their 40s, look at the lifestyle their parents are enjoying and wonder if they will be as fortunate as their folks.

"I don't have any idea if I'll have the money to support one household, much less two, thirty years from now when I'm in my seventies," says Jack, a 45-year-old father of four whose contracting business has suffered the peaks and valleys of the ever-changing economic conditions of the late 1980s and early 1990s.

His sister, Linda, agrees. "I'm a single parent. Every penny I make gets spent. And then some."

While both Jack and Linda know that their retirement years are fast approaching, neither feel as though they can do much to prepare financially for them right now. As for what they think their children can expect when they retire, the future picture looks fuzzy.

"I can't imagine what my life will be like in twenty years . . . much less try to figure out what my son's life will be like in fifty or sixty years. . . . What's that—in 2050?" says Linda. "Who can see that far ahead?"

How It Is Today

Even though the economic world continually changes, money still is money and is represented by a collection of handsomely decorated coins and paper bills that come in a variety of shapes and sizes and are used for one purpose—as a medium of exchange for goods and services.

On an emotional level, money may mean different things to different people: to some it represents self-worth or security; to others, power or success; and still others, the love of it is the root of all evil. But money, instead of gold coins, or buffalo hooves, or cat's tails, is the one thing we "exchange" when we want something: To get that Elton John CD I need to give the store clerk $12. That's how a money exchange works.

The curious thing about money is it knows not to whom it flows. Money doesn't know rich hands from poor hands, smart minds from ignorant ones, criminals from law-abiding citizens. It just circulates.

Every one of us needs money to live in our society, but when all is said and done, the amount of money we have—or don't have—may be a reflection of our net worth but has nothing to do with our individual self-worth.

Our Money Feelings

For most of us, what we feel, think, and teach our children about money is based upon what our parents felt, thought, and taught us. This fact, quite often, is the main reason many parents are reluctant to teach their kids anything about how to budget, save, acquire, or invest money: Not many of their parents taught them.

Once parents teach their children about saving places like piggy banks, cookie jars, and passbook savings accounts, that's often where the buck—and the children's financial education—stops. Psychologists say the reason for that is because parents are unsure about their own knowledge about money and therefore are afraid that they won't teach their kids the right things to do with it. So, they don't teach them much at all.

A Fine Example

It's estimated that currently children between the ages of 4 and 12 spend some $15 billion each year on everything from candy to clothes to videos. That's a lot of cash for kids to have control of—which is why it's so important for you to show and teach your kids about the ins and outs of the money exchange game.

Neal Cutler is a director of the Boettner Institute of Financial Gerontology at the University of Pennsylvania. He's been studying aging and money for years. As a father, Cutler knows all too well how hard it is to tune teenagers into retirement saving and planning. In an attempt to get his 17-year-old son's attention, Cutler wrote him a "birthday memo" explaining why it's important to financially plan ahead.

Here are some excerpts from the memo.*

Memorandum
To: Jori Lance Cutler
From: Your Dad

Well, son, you're a senior in high school now and it's time for another of those heavy father-son talks. I know it's awkward for both of us, but . . . let's talk retirement planning.

I know you've heard countless stories about how tough it was "back then." But on this issue of retirement, it's you who is likely to have the harder time of it unless you understand some of the fun-

*Journal of the American Society of CLD & ChFC, November 1992, pp. 36–39.

damentals of the wealth span, the impact of changes in the
American pension system on you, and compound interest.

Let's first consider some important questions and goals.
. . . When do you want to start your career as a full-time producer and
earner? How long do you want to work? That is, when do you think
you want to retire? Also, how long do you want to live in retirement?

These are tough questions to ponder, but take a look at the chart
below to see how they fit together. The chart is a simplified way of
looking at the overall human wealth-span and illustrates why an
early start to learning about retirement planning is so important.

People getting ready for retirement back in the 1930s started
working earlier, about age 20 or so. There wasn't much early retirement; they worked until about age 65, and average old-age life
expectancy was less than it is now. Consequently, for someone
approaching retirement in the 1930s, the accumulation stage was
fairly lengthy compared to the expenditure stage.

The wealth-span picture in the 1990s is quite different. Men and
women stay in school longer and start working later. What used to be
called "early retirement" is now normal, and on average we live a lot
longer in retirement. The outcome of all these demographic and economic changes is that the accumulations stage is shorter—and the
amount to be accumulated has to support a longer expenditure stage.

So now, son, let's answer those basic questions. There's a third line
in the chart that's labeled simply "You." Keep in mind as you choose
when to start work, when to retire, and how long you want or hope to
live in retirement that you are defining the accumulation stage and the
expenditure stage of your own personal wealth-span. . . .[See chart.]

The Human Wealth-Span

1930	0	10	20	30	40	50	60	70	80	90	100
1990	0	10	20	30	40	50	60	70	80	90	100
"YOU"	0	10	20	30	40	50	60	70	80	90	100

Accumulation Stage		Expenditure Stage

How much responsibility do you think you will personally have
for accumulating the assets you'll need during your expenditure
years? You might think that with Social Security and a good pension
your direct personal responsibility will be relatively small. . . . Not!

Don't worry about Social Security. It'll be around in one form or another, and anyhow, its goal traditionally has been to provide only the core of what you'll want to have in retirement. It's the traditional pension you should be concerned about. Back in the "good old days," most pensions were defined benefit pensions in which you were told in advance how much you would get per month when you retired. The better your salary and the longer you worked for your employer, the better your pension would be. . . .

But now there are more and more defined contribution plans. A major study reported earlier this year at the Pension Research Council of the University of Pennsylvania Wharton School concluded that the era of the defined benefit pension is waning . . . and most new pension plans are defined contribution plans. What does this have to do with the importance of your knowledge, understanding, and capacity to make informed investment choices?

Virtually everything.

In a defined contribution pension, the employer contributes some pension dollars, typically matching what you contribute from your pretax salary. The sum is placed into an account. . . . The basic responsibility for how this money is invested is yours. That is, what is guaranteed by your employer is the amount of the input, the contribution, and *not* the future value of the pension. This future value will be the result of a number of different choices that *you* will make, directly or indirectly. . . .

And it's not only money that's involved here, it's also temperament. We all know that money has a subjective, psychological quality as well as an objective "cold hard cash" quality. You have to be comfortable with the balance of return and risk that guides basic investment choices. You need to know how to diversify your hard-earned pension dollars into different investments. You should evaluate if, when, and how to work with your own investment adviser. And you should recognize early in life that your comfort level with different kinds of investments and risk will change over the course of your wealth-span. (Now that we talk about it, son, it looks like earning the money in the first place might be the easiest part of the process. Hanging on to it and making it grow for another thirty to forty years—now there's a challenge.) . . .

Probably the most important reason to see yourself in wealth-span terms and for seizing an early start in your accumulation stage is nothing more complicated than compound interest. We can discuss it more in detail another time, but for now let's look at a couple of examples. Suppose you deposited a penny in a bank account on the first day of the month, and on the second day the bank simply doubled it to 2 cents. On the third day they double it again to 4 cents, then to 8 cents, and so on. By the fifteenth of the month you would have $164, but by the end of one month you would have $5,368,709. Unfortunately, this bank couldn't sustain an interest rate of 100 percent per day and went out of business. But let's take a look at a more realistic example.

You were born in 1975 and so your first year of medical school will be in 1997. Let's assume an average interest rate of 7 percent per year over this period. If your mother and I had put $2000 into a special account on the day you were born and deposited the same amount on each of your first 7 birthdays but then stopped any new deposits, the persistent power of compound interest would produce a 1997 total of $61,000. But if we waited until your seventh birthday to make the first $2000 deposit but then kept on making them until 1997, these deposits, compounded at 7 percent, would total only $56,000.

In other words, by 1997 the earlier eight deposits totaling $16,000 produce a bottom line that is $5000 larger than the delayed 16 deposits totaling $32,000: ah, the power of compounding! In either case, I guess your first year's tuition is likely to be covered.

Well, Jori, that's it for now. Enclosed is your allowance. Don't invest it all in one place. . . .

Love,
Daddy

What You Can Do

Aesop has a couple of good fables that can teach children some basic money principles. The story of The Hare and the Tortoise with its moral that slow and steady wins the race is one way of teaching kids that it takes time for money to grow. It also teaches that persistence pays off.

Then there's the story of The Fox and the Goat. Its moral is look before you leap. Translated into a money lesson, whether you're spending, saving, or investing, you've got to understand where you're putting your money—before it gets spent or invested. That's a lesson we as adults seem to forever need to be reminded of. It's also rule number one if we are to be successful at money accumulation.

Once your kids are beyond the youngster stage, help them to understand all the different ways money can be used. If you're stuck for ideas, here are four suggestions:

1. If you pay your children an allowance, or when they receive money as gifts, tell them that they always will have choices about what to do with their money. Those choices usually are that money can either be saved, spent, or given away.

   You could even encourage your kids to divvy up their money into those three groupings. That way they will think more about what money is and consequently see that the managing of money means making decisions about what to do with it.

2. When your kids are old enough, have them sit down with you when you pay your monthly bills. This might take a little more

patience on your side, but actually showing kids how money flows in and out of their own household—plus on what and where it gets spent—is a tremendous way to show your children the realities of economic life.

3. Tell the truth about money. Teach your children that money does not grow on trees, some people have more money than others, not having money to spend does not mean you have no value as a human being, and that one of the wonderful things about our society is that not only are there a gazillion ways to make money, but that each of us is given the opportunity to be an entrepreneur if we choose to take that chance.

4. Show your children how money grows. You can do this by, instead of giving them a piggy bank, encouraging them to save their money in a clear glass jar. That way they can actually "see" the money mount up as they add to it.

Or, show them how the amount in your savings account grows as interest gets paid on it. And teach them about the magic of compounding.

Encouraging your kids to learn about money can pay off big-time for them in the future. All it takes is a little time and patience—the same two ingredients that make money grow.

Kids and Mutual Funds

If you're looking for a way to get your child interested in the stock market, there's a mutual fund that caters to children through its advertising literature and invests in the companies that make the products the kid in all of us seems to like.

Introduced in May 1994, the SteinRoe Young Investor Fund is a stock fund with a dual objective. First, its investing goal is to seek long-term capital appreciation, that is, make money grow. And second, the fund is intended to be a fun, educational experience for young investors and their parents.

"SteinRoe believes the best way to prepare the next generation for its financial future is to get them involved today," says Timothy K. Armour, president of SteinRoe Mutual Funds, a no-load fund family.

That fund family also knows that the kids market is a lucrative one. In 1994, for instance, the population of teenagers is expected to reach 25 million. Estimates for how much money those teens alone will spend hover around $89 billion. Plus SteinRoe says teenagers influence an additional $200 billion in purchases.

Add to that money factor the results of a 1993 Harris/Scholastic Research poll that asked 1389 students in grades 8 to 12 questions about their financial knowledge. When half of those polled said that they would like to take a class about money and investing, the stage was set for creating a mutual fund targeted at this audience.

Kenneth Corba was one of the team of three portfolio managers for this fund. Before going back to college and working on his MBA in the 1970s, Corba was a high school teacher. Always interested in education, he'd be happy if two things happened as a result of this fund.

"First, if we can provide an investment return that's superior to the S&P 500 so that we can have a really good investment experience, and second, if we can just emulate a sparkle or an interest in kids, getting them interested in following the stock market, following funds, and following companies. . . . That's all we're looking for."

According to Corba, the fund will have between 25 and 40 companies in its portfolio. And even though the fund intends to educate, the first criteria is to pick growth stocks for this fund that have investment merit.

Three of the stocks in that fund's portfolio in May 1994 were Procter & Gamble, the kids' connection here comes from the many products this company makes that young people use, like Crest toothpaste, Pampers diapers, and Clearasil blemish creams; Motorola, its wireless handheld telephones are a hit for kids of all ages; and Microsoft Corp., the leading software provider whose product line, Corba said, is growing to include an encyclopedia that kids will be able to access either through their own computers or via the TV.

The SteinRoe Young Investor Fund is also going to take some investing clues from its shareholders. Along with an investing kit that all shareholders will receive (this kit will include things like a coloring book for kids under age 7, a wall poster with spaces on it to fill in as investments are made into the fund, and a Young Investor Certificate), the fund plans on keeping an open line of communication with their investors by giving them an opportunity to write in suggestions to the portfolio managers about the products they like to buy.

"We are seriously going to take under consideration ideas that we get," says Corba.

To learn more about the SteinRoe Young Investor Fund and receive a pamphlet on commonly asked custodial account questions (a custodial account is one an adult opens for a minor), call 1-800-403-5437.

Twentieth Century, another mutual fund family, has a fund called the Twentieth Century Giftrust Investors. Investing into this fund takes a time commitment; all funds must be invested for at least 10 years. Monies, however, can be invested for longer periods of time. At the time the account is opened, you stipulate the time frame and date that you'd like the trust terminated.

People wanting to use the Giftrust as an investment for themselves, or to give as a gift to their children or anyone else, need only make an initial investment of $250. After that, the smallest amount of money you can add to the trust is $25.

Giftrust has been around since 1983, and while each year the performance of the fund goes up and down, for the past 11 years it has had an average annual return of over 21 percent. That means that $1000 invested in Giftrust at year-end 1983 would have been worth more than $8300 by year-end 1994; and a one-time investment of $10,000 would have grown in value to over $83,500 by the end of 1994.

Although the past performance of a mutual fund, or any other kind of investment, is not a guarantee of how such an investment will perform in the future, Giftrust's record is impressive.

For more information on the Twentieth Century Giftrust Investors, call 1-800-345-2021.

Custodial Accounts

There are literally hundreds of different mutual funds that will allow any adult to open a *custodial account* for a child and invest money in it on a regular monthly basis. Custodial accounts are technically called Uniform Gift to Minor Act (UGMA) or Uniform Transfer to Minor Act (UTMA) accounts.

For information on how to open a custodial account consult your broker or financial advisor. Or call Liberty Financial Companies at 1-800-403-KIDS and ask for a copy of their 50-page book titled *The Liberty Financial Young Investor Parent Guide*. It's free for the asking and I had a hand in writing it.

The booklet also offers general tips on teaching your kids about money, as well as basic information on different types of investments.

12
Women: Their Long, Hard Road to Retirement

Everything in the future is uncertain. Retirement planning can be a woesome ordeal affecting everybody differently and waking up some deeply hidden ghosts in each of our psyches—ones that for whatever reasons might prefer to be left alone sleeping. For women, the entire issue of retirement can be a particularly difficult one to face.

Many single and married women often look ahead to their golden years not with hopes and dreams and aspirations of spending their summer days gardening and winter ones in sunny Florida, California, or Arizona, but rather worrying about finances and what their chances are of becoming homeless. Women are particularly concerned about not having enough money to live comfortably in old age. For many maturing women, thinking into the future 20, 30, or 40 years winds up not being a whimsical way to while away an afternoon, instead it ends up being an experience they would rather avoid. But with smart foresight and planning, this picture can be totally changed. The straight talk about women and investing for their retirement can be summed up by these two reminders:

1. Women live longer than men.

2. On average, women earn less than men do.

Together, those two facts can spell disaster for the woman who does not take long-term financial planning seriously.

Who We Are

There are more women in the United States than there are men; more women are working in the 1990s than were in the 1980s; and close to two-thirds of the 100 million women age 16 and over are either working or looking for work as of 1994. Women have also accounted for 60 percent of the work-force growth between 1982 and 1992, and make up about 45 percent of all people working in the civilian work force—a figure that's projected to go to 47 percent by the year 2005.

Along with their strong and solid work-force presence, women generally outlive men: The U.S. Department of Health and Human Services says that today's typical 62-year-old man can plan on living to age 83 while a 62-year-old woman will live to age 90. And because women live longer than men, those over the age of 65 are almost three times as likely as men over 65 to be living alone.

As far as salaries are concerned, there are only about 400,000 women—or less than one-tenth of 1 percent of the population—who earn salaries of $75,000 per year or more. The Bureau of Labor Statistics reports that, on average, women earn 77 cents for every $1 men earn.

Even though females make up a powerful part of our nation's work force and outlive males, when it comes to managing money and/or investing for their retirement, most women are woefully undereducated.

Here's what a few of them have to say on the subject of retirement:

"When I was a young woman, I didn't think about retirement," says Catherine, a 42-year-old in Denver. "It never dawned on me that retirement was an issue in life that I'd have to deal with, much less have to save and prepare for financially."

"My mother used to always tell me to save my money," says a 78-year-old woman who's still a full-time employee. "I used to ask her, what for? Now I know what for."

"When people start talking to me about planning for my retirement and mention things like pensions and 401(k)s, I freeze up inside," confides a single woman, age 45, from Minneapolis, Minnesota. "I don't have a clue as to what they're talking about and feel too ashamed to admit it."

I too am one of the women who, up until recently, didn't think much about salting money away for my retirement. I figured that I'd get married and have a family, and hubby would take care of all the financial issues—like retirement. But guess what? I figured wrong.

Today not only am I the one making all the financial decisions in my household, I'm also the one who has to build her own retirement nest egg in record time. Like many of my baby-boomer pals, retirement is staring me straight in the face and I've done very little to save for it.

There is, however, hope. Women are an enduring sex with multiple talents. One of those talents is an ability to jump in and get a job done when the time calls for it.

Depending upon which sources you read, women either control most purse strings in the country or have little to no say in financial matters. I prefer to believe the first. Even the married woman who says she has absolutely no idea of how much money her husband makes, doesn't know whether she's in the will or not, and knows nothing about what, if any, investments he makes, generally has something to say about how money for both her home and her children gets spent. That may not be direct control over the family's purse strings, but it's control nonetheless.

There are reports too that say women make great investors; others that say they make horrible ones. Here again, I prefer the first. According to the National Association of Investors Corp. (NAIC), in Royal Oak, Michigan, female investors outperform male investors by 2 to 1, tend to shoot less from the hip than men do, and buy stocks at better prices than guys do.

Starting a Retirement Plan for Yourself

"In terms of retirement planning, women face the double-edged sword of earning less and living longer," says Jon S. Fossel, chairman and chief executive officer of Oppenheimer Management Corporation. "Their challenge is made even more formidable by their low savings rates and historical aversion to investment risk. A woman in America today can have fewer higher priorities than putting her financial house in order."

Getting your financial house in order begins with some simple ground rules.

Bridget Macaskill is president and chief operating officer of Oppenheimer Management Corporation, a mutual fund family that has created a lot of information and investment guides specifically designed for women. (To obtain any of this literature, simply call the Oppenheimer group at 1-800-525-7048 and request it.)

Macaskill says that there are four reasons why women need to become investors:

1. 65 percent of all marriages fail.
2. Women are widowed young. The average age of widowhood is 55.
3. 85 percent of women have no savings plan.
4. 48 percent of women fear that they'll become "bag ladies."

Armed with those statistics, if you are a married woman and have never had a retirement planning discussion with your husband, start one today. If you're a single woman, now is the time to begin creating a long-term retirement investment program for yourself if you've not done so already.

Some of the questions both you and your partner need to find out answers to include:

How much money do I make annually? How much does he?

Where does all that money go? (This can be a big task. Begin by sitting down and writing out where all the money that comes into your household in one month goes.)

Do we/I have a retirement plan?

If so, what is it?

How much money is in it?

Can we/I add more to it?

Who are the beneficiaries of my plan?

Does that plan meet our/my current—and projected—needs?

Where are the documents, records, and account numbers for all savings and retirement plans kept?

After you know where you stand, use that information to review your own, or your family's, financial situation. With that under your belt, you can start to confidently move ahead and make some concrete long-term financial plans.

Remember: If you're a female and feel as though you're all alone having to face the how-do-I-create-a-financial-nest-egg problem by yourself, you're not. You're in good company. Millions of us have a lot to learn about investing for our futures. Fortunately, we have a lot going for us! There is our keen survival instincts and intuitions, our willingness to learn, plus the fact that we generally think about and manage money differently than men do (and often more efficiently).

Studies show that women tend to think of money as a means to security whereas men tend to associate money with their own self-worth. Women are also more goal-oriented than men; willing to seek financial advice and guidance; and looking for long-term rather than short-term investments. But, most importantly, if you are among the large percentage of women who have not yet begun investing for your own retirement and are reading this book, you're probably willing to accept that challenge.

So no matter what your age, it's never too late to begin saving for your future. In fact, if you're 40 years old today, can invest $200 a month, do so faithfully each and every month for the next 25 years (until you're age 65), and let the money accumulate tax-deferred, earning an average of 8 percent per year, you'll have a nest egg that amounts to over $191,000 by the time you reach retirement age. If $100 per month is what your budget can allow, you'll still have over $95,000. And if you can invest $500 a month—using the same criteria—you'll have over $478,000. You see, this is all very doable—provided you start today.

Wealth Builder Tip_____

If you're divorced or considering that life change, there are lots of financial issues that need to be looked at.

The IRS has a pamphlet on the subject worth requesting. It is Publication 504, "Tax Information for Divorced and Separated Individuals."

Obtain a free copy by calling 1-800-829-3676.

PART 5

Putting It All Together

13

Juggling Three Balls: Social Security, Company Retirement Plans, and Your Own Portfolio

Planning for a secure retirement income from an investment point of view is a lot like a juggling act; you've got to keep three balls balancing in the air at all times to get the job done efficiently. Those three balls include Social Security and FICA taxes; employer-sponsored retirement plans; and building your own retirement portfolio independent of those other two programs.

Here's how each ball can work to provide you with a retirement income.

Ball 1: Social Security

As you learned earlier, Social Security can play a big part in your monthly income once you have retired or if you're over age 70 and still working. But keep in mind these two points: (1) it is unlikely that those benefits alone will be enough to support your preretirement lifestyle and (2) odds are you will receive Social Security benefits only if you've worked for them.

Knowing precisely how much money you, as a retiree, will receive in Social Security income benefits becomes more and more important the closer you get to retiring. So, as you near retirement age, make sure to contact the Social Security Administration office to get an idea of how much your monthly checks could amount to.

As we mentioned earlier, even if calculations reveal that your Social Security benefits will make up a relatively low percentage of your projected retirement income, most of us can't afford to miss out on the income that this particular ball can provide.

Ball 2: What Your Boss Offers

While the subject of retirement may be a popular one, employees don't always understand what, if any, kinds of retirement benefit plans their employers offer. If you're not familiar with any of your company's benefits packages, ask your boss about them today. Or visit the human services or corporate benefits coordinator of your company and ask for assistance. Taking full advantage of the qualified retirement plan your employer offers is a must if you'd like to retire with the maximum benefits possible.

Ball 3: Your Own Creation

The third ball we've all got to keep in the air is the one pertaining to our own individual savings/investing plan. That's the one in which we invest on our own, independent of the FICA tax we pay and the retirement programs we participate in at work.

This ball is especially important for the self-employed and those not covered by a pension plan at work. If you fall into either category, sit down today with paper and pencil in hand, look at the money you've got coming into your household, and make it a point to start saving.

The record shows that it's the rewards from your personal savings and investment portfolios that make living the really good life in retirement possible. In fact, for high-income wage earners, it's not

Social Security that provides them with their greatest source of monthly income, or their company's retirement plans, but the returns from their own personal portfolios.

The quickest way to begin building the savings portion of this ball is to start with the basics, namely you and your own personal needs.

To start saving for your retirement, consider these three points:

1. How much time do I have to save for my retirement?

2. What's my investing personality like?

3. How much money can I put into a retirement savings program today?

The answers to these three questions will do two things. First, they will help you to zero in on what kinds of retirement products might be appropriate for you. Second, they will aid you in the creation of a retirement nest egg—not a goose egg.

How Much Time Do I Have Before I Retire?

There is no doubt about it, the sooner you begin saving and/or investing money, the better the chances are that you can build a nice financial nest egg for yourself. But talking about saving and investing and doing either are two different things.

"We all say that we're going to put money away for our retirement, but how many of us actually do?" asks Julie Russell, a stockbroker in West Palm Beach, Florida. "There always seems to be something that we'd rather spend our money on today . . . other than retirement, that is."

And Russell's right. For most of us, buying a new car, saving for a new sound system, or taking a month-long trip to Southern France seem like far better ways of spending our money today than, say, socking it into a retirement account for tomorrow does.

Unfortunately, spending all of our money today doesn't help us if our goal is to build up assets to spend during our later years. This brings us to the first, and last, rule of retirement investing; Set some timely goals.

In your personal savings sphere it's best to invest for three different time frames; the short, medium, and long term. Here's a very conservative investment strategy outline to use as a guide for how you might want to divvy up money among these three categories:

- *Short-term goals.* This is emergency money, today money, rainy-day money, comfort-zone money, feel-good money. It's money you can get your hands on. How much of it you need to accumulate depends upon what your lifestyle expenses and housekeeping needs are. To build this pot of gold, set up a savings or money-market account, either through your own bank or credit union. Vacation savings and Christmas or gift spending could be a part of these short-term needs fund, too. Adding to this short-term pot is essential. It's from this base that all other investment monies are likely to come because once this pot gets big enough, you can draw from it to make medium- and long-term investments.

- *Medium-term goals.* Saving for a downpayment for a home, a car, or any other big-ticket items that will take more than one year but less than, say, five, six, or seven to accumulate, is what medium-term savings goals are all about.

- *Long-term goals.* Your kids' future educations and your own retirement or other goals 8, 10, 20, or more years in the future make up this category.

Now that you've got an understanding of these three different time-frame goals, here are some investment ideas for each category:

1. For short-term goals, invest conservatively. Money-market funds, savings accounts, CDs, and short-maturing Treasury bills and short-maturing bonds are all examples of conservative investments.

2. For medium-term goals, invest moderately. One conservative medium-term investment strategy would be to create a bond portfolio made up of bonds with various maturity dates. To do that, save up, say, $5000, and break the money into five chunks, each $1000 in size. Then invest $1000 into a CD, Treasury, or highly rated corporate or tax-free bond that matures in one year; another $1000 into one maturing in two years; and so on down the line until you've invested the entire $5000 into securities all maturing one year after another. If $5000 is too much, try saving $500. Once that goal is attained, break that amount into five $100 groups and invest each into CDs that mature at various times. Using this strategy allows money to mature each year. That money can then be reinvested again at the current rates to keep the ladder going. Or it can be used for something else.

Investing in high-quality stocks or stock funds can also be a moderate investing choice. Balanced funds that invest in both stocks and bonds or in blue-chip stocks are two types of funds often ranked as moderate-risk. But be careful here. If you know that your money is only going to be invested in a stock mutual fund for under five years, remember that markets run in cycles and, depending upon which part of the cycle you invest in, you may or may not get back all the money initially invested. Also, if the fund selected is one with a sales charge, it can take a few years to recover the cost of that fee, depending upon the performance of that fund.

3. For long-term investing, the pros say be aggressive, if you can. Here, growth or value stocks or stock funds—like aggressive, growth, value, international, and global funds—are the investment choices most often suggested.

If you're a little gun-shy of investing aggressively and want to minimize the risk of your principal investment into long-term securities, consider hedging your long-term aggressive stock portfolio by purchasing zero-coupon bonds that are held until they mature. Zero-coupon bonds are sold at discounts to their face value and can be used to complement a long-term investing plan. Here's how: Let's say that you have $5000 to invest for 20 years and would like to put that money into a stock fund. To make sure that in 20 years you'll get back at least $5000, ask your broker to find out what the cost of a $5000 face value, noncallable, triple-A-rated zero-coupon bond that matures in 20 years would be. Costs for these bonds are similar to those of Series EE bonds—in that they are sold at deep discounts to their face value. Which means, if that zero-coupon bond costs, say, $1500, buy it, and invest the remaining $3500 into the stock fund of your choice, and hold each for 20 years. At that time the bond will mature, returning you the original $5000; whatever monies the stock fund has made is all gravy.

No matter what your long-term aggressive investment choices may be, the secrets to any successful long-term investing are simple: One, use common sense, and two, only invest in products—or investment strategies—you understand.

What's Your Investment Personality?

The accounting firm of KPMG Peat Marwick identifies two basic personality types: savers and investors. Here's what they say about each:

Savers:

Protect their safety of principal

Minimize the risk in interest/principal fluctuations

Minimize the variability of returns they receive

Emphasize income in their portfolios

Accept little or no protection from inflation

Like to maintain liquid portfolios

Investors:

Like to see their money grow

Accept the risks of interest/principal fluctuations

Accept variable returns from their investments

Emphasize appreciation rather than return

Protect principal from inflationary erosion

Have diversified portfolios of securities.

Ideally, anyone investing for her or his retirement needs to blend those two personality profiles together, choosing some investments that offer fixed kinds of returns and others offering variable ones.

But savers beware! Money pro Jonathan Pond offers this warning for long-term investors choosing only to place their money in low-risk investment options:

> CDs, money-market deposit accounts, money-market mutual funds, savings accounts, Treasury bills, U.S. savings bonds, and so on, all have one drawback to them. That is, after you have paid income tax on the interest, you've probably lost ground to inflation. And over time this can significantly erode the purchasing power of your investments.

To get an inkling of what your investment tolerance is, if your stomach gets tied up in knots every time you hear about changes in stock market prices, or if you need to call your broker for stock prices two or three times a day, or you check the prices on your mutual funds daily, chances are you're not the buy-it-and-forget-it type of investor.

While saving money for many of us is anxiety-free, investing it might not be. So, if you're a nervous Nellie or someone who doesn't want to take a lot of risk with the money you are saving for retirement or someone who finds that investing literally makes you sick, don't invest. But do at least double up on the amount of money that you save for no other reason than to cover the long-term effects of inflation. And don't forget about the potential long-term costs of a conservative approach to savings.

RISK TEST

Here's a five-question quiz that won't take much time to complete and will give you an indication of how much risk you're willing to take when it comes to investing.

1. You're the winner on a television game show! Which prize would you pick?
   A. $2000 in cash
   B. A 50 percent chance to win $4000
   C. A 20 percent chance to win $10,000
   D. A 2 percent chance to win $100,000

2. You're down $500 in a poker game. How much more would you bet to get the $500?
   A. More than $500
   B. $500
   C. $250
   D. $100
   E. Nothing—you'll cut your losses now

3. One month after another you buy a stock. It rises 15 percent. You would:
   A. Hold it, hoping for more gains
   B. Sell it and take your gains right now
   C. Buy more shares, as it could go higher

4. You're a key employee in a start-up company. Pick one of these ways to take your year-end bonus:
   A. $1500 in cash
   B. Stock options that could bring you $15,000 next year if the company succeeds, nothing if it fails

5. A stock drops 15 percent a month after you invest. Its fundamentals still look good. What would you do?
   A. Buy more—if it looked good at the original price, it looks even better now
   B. Hold on and wait for it to come back
   C. Sell to avoid losing even more

Answers:

Question 1: If you chose *A*, give yourself 1 point; *B*, 3 points; *C*, 5 points; and *D*, 9 points.

Question 2: If you chose *A*, give yourself 8 points; *B*, 6 points; *C*, 4 points; *D*, 2 points; and *E*, 1 point.

Question 3: If you chose *A*, give yourself 3 points; *B*, 1 point; *C*, 4 points.

Question 4: If you chose *A*, give yourself 1 point; *B*, 5 points.

Question 5: If you chose *A*, give yourself 4 points; *B*, 3 points; and *C*, 1 point.

Scoring: If you scored 5 to 18 points, you may be a more conservative investor. Your investment should have high credit ratings and well-established records of stability.

If you scored 19 to 30 points, you're willing to take more chances to achieve greater rewards. In choosing investments, look for higher returns. You may be a candidate for bonds with higher yields and lower bond ratings, or stocks of newer companies.

SOURCE: T. Rowe Price Associates, PBPost, May 3, 1993, page 10, Business Monday.

How Much Money Can I Put into a Retirement Savings Plan Now?

There is money that comes into your household every month whether you're on welfare, are a nonworking person, or the CEO at a major corporation. So to say you have no money isn't usually the truth. We all have money crossing our palms in some fashion during a month's period of time.

The trick to saving money is not to spend it all. So the answer to how much money you have to save or invest right now is a matter of money management. No matter how much money you manage each month, you can afford to save some. Believe me. Even if all you can save is a quarter a week, or a dollar a week, or five dollars a week. Whatever. Just save money. Saving money is a habit—and a good one to get into. Saved money grows until it gets spent.

If you're not saving any money today, get into the habit and try this: Out of each and every paycheck you receive, or of all the money that comes into your household monthly, set aside a certain amount, or percentage, for you. Save that money. Then once you've gotten into the savings habit, create some short-, medium-, and long-term savings/investing goals. Investing a portion of your money is essential if you hope to live in your retirement years in the style you dream of. So like the ad says, just do it.

Opportunity Costs

Everything in life seems to come with a price tag, a cost. It's sort of an "if I do that, then the consequences to me will be . . ." kind of thing. Even investors aren't exempt from it.

Those who aggressively invest in stocks and bonds quickly come to understand that the price of a stock can go up just as easily as it can go down. Bond investors who decide to sell their bonds before the bonds' maturity date learn how the movements up and down of interest rates affect the price of a bond. And people who keep their money stashed in a coffee can at home realize that even though the money is in a safe place, it isn't working for them as it would be if it were in an interest-bearing account.

For the very conservative investor there is a cost to that money management style—one that financial experts refer to as an *opportunity cost*.

"Investing for safety can carry a cost that investors often overlook," says Steve Schoepke, senior analyst of mutual funds at Moody's Investor Service. "That cost is what economists refer to as an 'opportunity' cost."

Schoepke explained that an opportunity cost results when investors choose low-risk/low-return investments and thereby miss out on the opportunity of receiving higher returns from riskier investments.

Of course there are never any guarantees to the kinds of returns higher-risk investments will bring, but investing a portion of your investment cash in what you might consider "riskier investments" is what opportunity costs are all about. It's also part and parcel of what the notion of "diversification" refers to—namely, that you don't put all your eggs into one basket of securities. And for the safety-minded investor, keeping all your money in short-term investment products, like CDs or money-market funds, isn't diversifying, it's putting all your money into the same kinds of products: short-term fixed-income ones.

Schoepke pointed out that for those who decide to keep their money in safe investments such as money-market funds, there is minimal chance of losing any of the money they've invested. But should those investors move their monies into the world of stock, bond, and long-term mutual fund investing, "the likelihood of loss associated with riskier investments diminishes" the longer one holds onto their investments.

In other words, in the risky investment arena, risk is often highest over the short run rather than during the long term.

Table 13-1 was created by Schoepke to demonstrate how risk and reward vary between money-market funds and a stock or stock fund over various time periods. "Understanding and taking these relationships into

Table 13-1. How Risk and Reward Vary between Money-Market and Stock Funds

	Various holding periods		
	1 Year	10 Years	20 Years
Money Market Funds			
Probability of losing principal	0%	0%	0%
Opportunity cost vs. stock	Low	Medium	High
Stock or Stock Funds			
Probability of losing principal	30%	4%	0%
Opportunity cost vs. money funds	High	Medium	Low

account when investing for retirement is especially important," says Schoepke. "The reason for this is that for many, retirement investing is synonymous with investing over a long holding period of time."

What that translates to is: Because retirement savings is generally a long-term proposition, the probability of losing your original "risky" investment's dollar amount goes down the longer you hold on to it.

Looked at another way, Schoepke's point is simply this: If, for instance, you're going to invest in the stock market and plan on buying a few stocks—or even a few stock funds—plan on holding those investments for decades, not days.

Opportunity cost therefore, isn't a short-term notion, it's for long-term planners—like for those saving for their retirement.

Diversification: Two Reds, Two Blues, Two Greens

Diversification in your investment portfolio is like variety in life; both add spice.

A diversified retirement plan is one that invests in a variety of things and among a variety of asset classes. In the stock market that could mean investing in stocks, bonds, and mutual funds. Outside of Wall Street it might mean putting your money into real estate and antique cars.

Diversification, in other words, is the "and" not the "or" in the investment choices we make.

Understanding diversification begins with realizing (1) what an asset is, and (2) what an asset class is.

An *asset* is anything you own that has value. Stocks, bonds, and mutual funds are assets. So are cash, CDs, and your home—as are real estate and collectibles like artwork, jewelry, and rare coins.

An *asset class* has a broader meaning and lumps the same kinds, or types, of assets together. For instance, if you own three different pieces of property—a rental home, a commercial building, and a vacant lot—you may feel as though your investments are diversified, but in reality all three of those properties are part of the same class of assets, that is, real estate.

If you're a fan of mutual funds and own shares of a blue-chip fund, an international equity fund, and a small-company growth fund, while your portfolio of mutual funds is diversified, it's not diversified among asset classes; all of those three funds are equity, or stock, funds.

Frequently, people keep their money in CDs at a variety of banks believing that since they've spread their money among different banking institutions, they've also spread their investment risks. That's not so. Buying the same kind of investment, in this case CDs, and buying them at different banks isn't spreading the risk, it's simply spreading your money around in the same asset class of investments at different banks.

An easy way of understanding asset classes and how important it is to cross-invest among them is to think of them as you would the various food groups that we are supposed to eat in order to maintain a healthy diet. In your mind's eye, visualize a refrigerator, one in a well-stocked kitchen. Then imagine opening its door and looking at all the different kinds of foods inside. Picture among the shelves and storage bins items like milk, eggs, and cheese; soda pop, juices and maybe some beer or wine; steak, chicken, or fish; fruits and vegetables; and maybe even some leftovers and sweets.

Refrigerators like the one just imagined are chock-full of a variety of different kinds of foods, each representing different food groups, with each food group vital to maintaining a healthy body. Common sense tells us that eating one type of food like dairy products alone, each day and every day, is no way to maintain a healthy body. Neither would be eating only vegetables all day long, day in and day out. So, if you think of asset classes as food groups, you can see why the "health" of your investment portfolio depends to a large degree on how diversified it is.

Investing across Asset Classes

"One of the things that I've learned while being out on the road," says John Silvia, chief economist at Kemper Financial Services, "is that a lot of people got out of their CDs and thought they were diversifying by buying a government bond fund. Well, that's not really diversification."

The investment risks of both CDs and bond fund investing revolve around movements in interest rates. So while someone may think he's got a healthy—truly diversified—portfolio of securities because he owns a few CDs along with some shares of a bond fund, his diversification is only within the same asset class—fixed income.

Silvia said that real diversification means crossing asset classes. In other words, you should own some CDs, along with shares of stock or stock funds.

Ideally, then, a diversified retirement portfolio will be one in which both income-producing investments as well as growth opportunity investments are made. Because investments don't all perform the same at all times, one of the best ways to ensure that your investments work for you over the long haul is to spread out the risk of investing among the different asset classes. That means investing in stocks, for their growth potential and ability to outperform inflation, and in bonds or income-producing securities, for their steady constant return.

Having said that, many people aren't comfortable investing among the different asset classes and prefer to keep their money in a savings account in a bank that's FDIC-insured. Or they prefer to keep it only in CDs. If your investment psyche won't permit you to take chances with any of the money that you've saved, that's OK, too. Money saved is far better than money not saved or foolishly invested.

What's Asset Allocation?

Asset allocation is the "how much" part of your long-term financial investing equation—how much you have invested in each of the various asset classes like stocks, or bonds, or CDs, or gold, or real estate, or antique cars, or whatever. For example, if you have three different IRAs, each one invested in CDs maturing at various times, 100 percent of your asset allocation is in one asset class—fixed income. But if one of those IRAs was invested in an emerging growth mutual fund, one in a bond fund, and one in CDs maturing in five years, your asset allocation would be one-third in equities and two-thirds in fixed-income investments.

Remember, every time you add something to or subtract something from your retirement plan you've changed the asset mix.

What's important to remember about asset allocation is:

1. *Nothing stays the same.* As you grow older, or as your income changes, or as your life needs change or the assets in your home and retirement accounts change, so does the way in which you've allocated your assets.

2. *Mix it up—consistently.* Be sure to invest across product lines and invest in instruments that meet your own personal time horizons and investment objectives, and keep this rhythm going throughout your life.

3. *Reallocate on purpose.* Creating a long-term retirement plan is one thing; converting those investments into usable dollars the nearer you get toward retirement age as well as during retirement is another. So, like a will that needs to be updated periodically throughout your lifetime, your retirement assets need periodic adjusting, too.

Choosing an Asset Allocation

Trying to decide how to divvy up your money is challenging. It's challenging because just as our lives change as we live them, markets change year in and year out. So coming up with a definitive asset allocation mix that will last a lifetime is something few could accurately recommend.

But, aside from keeping 100 percent of your money in cash, 100 percent invested in the stock market, or 100 percent invested in bonds, one way of deciding where your money is invested can be determined by your age and your investment objectives.

Table 13-2, from the Vanguard Group, a mutual fund family in Valley Forge, Pennsylvania, will give you an idea of some of the differ-

Table 13-2. Asset Allocation

Retirement (your age)	Recommended asset allocation	Historic returns*
20–49	Growth— 80% Stocks 20% Bonds	+ 9.6%
50–59	Balanced growth— 60% Stocks 40% Bonds	+ 8.6%
60–74	Conservative growth— 40% Stocks 40% Bonds 20% Cash reserves	+ 7.4%
75+	Income— 20% Stocks 60% Bonds 20% Cash reserves	+ 6.2%

*Average annual returns for 1926 to 1993.

SOURCE: The Vanguard Group and *Stocks, Bonds, Bills, and Inflation, 1994 Yearbook,* Ibbotson Associates, Chicago (annually updated by Roger G. Ibbotson and Rex A. Singuefield). Used with permission. All rights reserved.

Table 13-3. Performance of Different Portfolios of Stocks and Bonds during Years 1945–1993*

Portfolio	No. of down years	Average loss in down year, %	Worst 1-year loss, %	Average annual return, %
Aggressive: 100% stocks	11	− 9.4	− 26.5	11.7
Growth: 75% stocks, 25% bonds	9	− 7.2	− 18.4	10.5
Balanced: 50% stocks, 50% bonds	8	− 4.0	− 10.4	9.1
Income: 75% bonds, 25% stocks	5	− 1.5	− 2.7	7.6
Conservative: 100% bonds	5	− 0.7	− 1.3	5.9

*Figures are based on Ibbotson Associates data for the Standard & Poor's 500 stock index and intermediate-term bonds.
SOURCE: T. Rowe Price Associates. Printed in *The Wall Street Journal*, April 8, 1994, p. c1.

ent ways you can mix up your assets according to your age and investment objectives. Use it as a guide, not as gospel.

The Past Performance of Some Typical Asset Mixes

Long-term investors have to be able to handle price changes in both the stock and bond markets over time. Exactly how those prices will fluctuate, however, is anybody's guess.

Table 13-3 shows how different portfolios' blends of stocks and bonds performed in the years from 1945 to 1993.

An Investment Plan Checklist

Here's a checklist to run through that will give you an idea of what kinds of long-term retirement plans you currently have in place and how much is invested in each.

Once you've completed the checklist, take a look at it every year or so and update it. That way you'll keep abreast of how well your long-term investing plans are working.

Filling in the checklist will, hopefully, put you in a long-term investing mode, help you to conceptualize some goals, and get you looking for investment products that can match your investment needs.

One final thought: While there are no guarantees when it comes to investing, there are ways to minimize the risks involved. One centers around time and matching up your personal needs with the appropriate investment products. Another asks us to be flexible. Both play essential roles in our long-term retirement plans.

Social Security

yes____no____ Have you paid in the appropriate amount in FICA taxes and worked the appropriate number of quarters to qualify for Social Security benefits?

If you don't know the answer to this question, call the Social Security Administration at 1-800-772-1213 and ask for their informational packet describing how Social Security benefits work. (See Chapter 7 for more information on Social Security.)

Company Qualified Retirement Plans

yes____no____ Does the company that you work for offer its employees a qualified retirement plan?

yes____no____ If so, are you participating in that program?

What kind of qualified plan does your company offer its employees?

_____defined benefit

_____defined contribution

Who is responsible for deciding how the monies in your qualified retirement plan are invested?

_____you

_____your boss

_____both of you

yes____no____ Do you know how your retirement monies are invested in your company's retirement plan?

List the types or kinds of investments in your employer-sponsored retirement account and then check off the kinds of risk levels you believe each investment to be.

Name of investment	Risk: low/medium/high
_____	_____
_____	_____
_____	_____

yes____no____ Do you need to be vested in your employer-sponsored retirement plan to be able to take full advantage of all of its benefits?

yes____no____ If you answered "yes" to the last question, are you fully vested in the program yet?

Note: If you are not fully vested, find out what your current status is in that program. If you don't know how to do that, ask your company's benefit plans coordinator.

yes____no____ If you're a part of a defined contribution employer-sponsored retirement plan such as a 401(k), and you were to leave that job and move into another, do you know how much of the money that you contributed to your 401(k) would move with you?

yes____no____ When changing jobs, are you familiar with the appropriate way to roll over retirement account monies so you can avoid tax penalties?

Individual Retirement Plans

yes____no____ Do you have one or more IRAs?

If you answered "yes" to the last question, write down the answers to the following questions:

What are your IRAs invested in (CDs, stocks, stock funds, etc.)? Where are those IRAs held (at a bank, brokerage firm, or fund family)?

Investment product	Where held
_____	_____
_____	_____
_____	_____

To get an idea of how diversified your IRA investments are, answer the following three questions.

1. How much money did you originally invest in each of your IRAs?

_____

_____

_____

_____

2. How much has that investment changed in value? (For example, if you invested $1000 in an IRA, in individual stocks, or in stock or bond mutual funds in 1989, multiply the number of shares of each investment that you have now with their current price per share to find out how much money your original investment is worth today. Or if your IRAs are invested in CDs, write down what each is now worth.)

_____

_____

_____

_____

3. Indicate type of investment by writing "fixed" for IRA investments placed into products that provide fixed rates of returns, like CDs and individual bonds do, and "variable" for those IRA investments on which the returns go up and down, as they would if you'd invested in stocks or stock and bond funds.

_____

_____

_____

_____

Retirement Plans for the Self-Employed

Self-employed people need to be doubly conscious of making long-term retirement investing plans. After all, they are their own bosses, and as such they are the only ones responsible for providing a qualified retirement plan for themselves. So, if you are your own boss and answer "no" to the next three questions, you might want to strongly consider making IRA, SEP-IRA, or Keogh investing a part of your annual budget plan.

yes_____no_____ Do you have an IRA?

yes_____no_____ Do you have an SEP-IRA?

yes_____no_____ Do you have a Keogh?

If you've answered "yes" to any of these questions, fill out the following:

IRA, SEP-IRA, or Keogh
investment product   Where held

_____   _____

_____   _____

_____   _____

To get an idea of how diversified your investments are, answer the following three questions in the space provided at the end of question 3:

1. How much was the original amount of money you placed into each SEP-IRA and/or Keogh account?

2. How much has that investment changed in value? (For example, if you invested $1000 in individual stocks or stock or bond mutual funds in 1991, multiply the number of shares of each investment that you have now by its current price per share to find out how much money your original investment is currently worth. Or if these retirement accounts were invested in CDs, write down what each is now worth.)

3. Is the return on these investments fixed or variable? (Write "fixed" for SEP-IRA and/or Keogh investments placed into products that provide fixed rates of return, such as CDs and individual bonds, and "variable" for those in which the returns go up and down, as they would if you'd invested in stocks or stock and bond funds.)

Original investment   What its value is today   Fixed or variable
_____

_____

_____

_____

_____

_____

Personal Savings / Investments

yes_____ no_____ Do you have a savings account?

yes_____ no_____ Do you own CDs?

yes_____ no_____ Do you own U.S. savings bonds?

yes_____ no_____ Do you have a savings account at your credit union?

yes_____ no_____ Have you created an investment portfolio outside of your retirement plans? (Examples are owning stocks or bonds outside of those that may be in any qualified retirement accounts, real estate as an investment, and precious metals or artwork as investments.)

If you've answered "yes" to any of these questions, answer the following question, then in the allotted spaces list each investment type and state where it is held:

Where are your personal savings invested? And where do you keep things like the certificates, deeds, or the valuables themselves?

Investment   Where held

_____   _____

_____   _____

_____   _____

_____   _____

_____   _____

The Big Picture

Now let's take a look at all the investments that you've made, what their market value is today, and whether their returns are fixed or variable. To do that, look back at what you've written on the preceding pages and reenter that information in the chart that follows.

For example, if you are participating in your company's 401(k) plan and those monies are in the Magellan stock fund, enter "401(k) Magellan Fund" under the "Retirement Plan" heading, enter the current market value of that investment under "Today's Market Value," and enter "Varied" under "Fixed or Variable."

Retirement plan or other retirement investment	Today's market value	Fixed or variable?

14

More about Inflation and Taxes

Question: At what rate will I be taxed on the income I get from my retirement accounts?

Answer: Great question. And one without a single answer.

The thinking behind deferring taxes, which means paying them at a later date, centers around two notions. The first is that presumably, after retirement your annual income will be lower than your income is today. The second is that the percentage of tax on your income will be lower than it is today.

If both are true—if your annual income is lower when you retire than it is today, and the level at which you are taxed is also—then tax-deferred investing makes good sense. But if tax rates climb, there is a chance the level at which your income is taxed during retirement might be higher than the one you're subject to today.

Tax rates in this country have fluctuated greatly during this century. And because nobody can foresee what the tax rates will be in the future, and more specifically when you retire, there is no definite answer to this question today.

Question: Will my retirement income be all tax-free?

Answer: In the words of Eliza from *My Fair Lady,* "Wouldn't that be loverly?"

More often than not, any distributions received from qualified retirement plans—such as from IRAs, 401(k)s, 403(b)s, or profit-sharing plans—are all subject to income tax—with *one* exception.

That exception is if the money that funded the retirement account was an "after-tax" contribution. In other words, if you already had paid income tax on the money funding your retirement account, you won't have to pay taxes on that money again—however, you will have to pay on the capital gains the investments may have provided.

A circumstance like that could arise if you were participating in your company's 401(k) or 403(b) plan, contributing the maximum you could to that account, and, in an effort to build as fat a nest egg as possible, were also funding an IRA each year with monies that taxes had already been paid on. If that's the case, the IRA money would not be subject to taxes when it was withdrawn, but the interest or capital gains it earned would be taxable.

To make sure you don't wind up in a double-tax situation regarding your retirement accounts:

- Keep accurate records of every different retirement account that you participate in.
- Specify how much money was contributed to each and when those contributions were made.
- Designate whether money contributed was pretax or after-tax dollars.

This kind of record keeping is a *must do!*

To Defer or Not to Defer?

To defer or not to defer? Now there's something to think about.

As we pointed out earlier, the thinking behind investing into products that defer taxes (deferring means not paying taxes on an investment until a later date) is based on the concept that any income received during retirement will be taxed at a lower rate than it is today.

But, if the income tax rates of the past are any indication of what the income tax rates will be in the future, that kind of thinking could prove to be full of hot air. And it could cost you money.

On the other hand, it's hard to argue with the fact that money, left untouched to compound and grow tax-deferred, can grow like dandelions in a lawn. (For a perfect example, look back at the chart in Chapter 5, "Why Participate?")

The key, of course, to answering the question "Which is better, tax-deferred retirement investments or ones in which taxes are paid as they come along?" is, again, diversification.

Cover as many bases as you possibly can with monies earmarked for your retirement. That is, why not keep some of your retirement monies in investments in which the taxes on them are paid annually and the remainder in ones that are tax-deferred.

What kinds of products are tax-deferred investments? Any products selected to fund your retirement accounts will turn into tax-deferred investments once they are in an IRA, 401(k), Keogh, and so on.

Some investments in which taxes would have to be paid each year would be any monies you have in your personal savings account or money-market accounts; or interest and dividend income from the individual stocks and bonds that you own; or the monies that your company pays out to you from their profit-sharing plans.

SOME LUMP-SUM DISTRIBUTION OPTIONS

A *lump-sum distribution* is money that represents your share of a qualified retirement plan and comes to you either when changing jobs or at retirement.

While the notion of receiving this financial windfall may seem exciting, deciding what to do with the money always means reviewing the tax implications. The table on pages 162–163 is taken from the booklet *Receiving a Lump-Sum Distribution: A Guide for Investors Aged 50 and Over* and provides some ideas of what choices there are regarding lump-sum distributions.

For a copy of the entire pamphlet, call The AARP Investment Program from Scudder at 1-800-322-2282.

Lump-Sum Distributions

When Bill Lenar decided to change jobs, one of the questions he had to face was what to do with all the monies that had accumulated in his retirement plan. His choice was either to take the money in one lump sum or transfer it into another qualified retirement account like an IRA.

Bill's decision got a whole lot easier to make once he looked into what the tax consequences of each were.

Some Lump-Sum Distribution Options

Option	Benefits	Investment choices	Cautions	Tax considerations
IRA (transfer or rollover)	■ Wide range of investment choices ■ Tax-deferred ■ Beneficiary allowed ■ Conduit IRA holds distribution until it is rolled back into qualified plan ■ Immediate access to your money without IRS early withdrawal penalty, if you base distributions on life expectancy ■ Money, in most other plans [401(k)s, 403(b)s, etc.] qualify for IRA transfers or rollovers	■ Wide range of choices, including mutual funds, CDs, stocks, bonds, annuities ■ Can't invest in gold or collectibles	■ Can't use your money as collateral for a loan ■ Must start taking distributions by age 70½ ■ For large balance accounts, possible IRS penalties when distributions begin, or at death ■ For rollovers, 20% withheld for taxes; withholding is taxed and penalized as a distribution if not rolled over ■ Rollovers must be made within 60 days	■ No IRS early withdrawal penalty on money transferred or rolled over ■ Money in IRA account grows tax-deferred ■ For rollovers, 20% withheld for taxes; withholding is taxed and penalized as a distribution if not rolled over
Qualified plans (leave in present plan; transfer or rollover)	■ Tax-deferred ■ Forward averaging and capital gain tax treatments may be used when lump-sum distribution is taken ■ Beneficiary allowed ■ Some plans allow you to borrow from your account	■ Choices limited to those offered by the plan ■ Some plans offer special investment options, such as employer stock	■ Not all qualified plans will accept a transfer or rollover ■ Generally, must start taking distributions by age 70½ ■ Assets in this plan can't be used as collateral for a loan outside the plan	■ Money in qualified plan account grows tax-deferred ■ No IRS early withdrawal penalty on money kept in employer's plan or transferred or rolled over to another qualified plan ■ For rollovers, 20% withheld for taxes; withholding

Pay taxes on money now

- Immediate access to your money
- If you were born before January 1, 1936, and you were a plan participant for five years, you may be able to use 5- or 10-year averaging, and capital gains treatment for pre-1974 portion of your pension
- If you are age 59½, and you were a plan participant for five years, you can use five-year averaging

- Spend or invest your money any way you like.

- For rollovers, 20% withheld for taxes; withholding is taxed and penalized as a distribution if not rolled over
- Rollovers must be made within 60 days
- Must pay taxes the year you keep your distribution
- 20% of distribution withheld for taxes
- Earnings on your money taxed each year (unless you invest in tax-free investments such as municipal bonds)
- Money can never be transferred or rolled over to an IRA or qualified plan
- Taxes reduce power of compounding
- If you are under age 59½, you may have to pay 10% IRS early withdrawal penalty

- is taxed and penalized as a distribution if not rolled over
- Immediate taxes on full amount of your money
- 20% of distribution withheld for taxes
- Earnings on the money taxed annually (unless you invest in tax-free investments such as municipal bonds)
- Future annual earnings on this money will be added to your other income, possibly raising your tax bracket

SOURCE: The AARP Investment Program from Scudder.

His accountant advised him that if he were to take the lump-sum distribution in full, taxes would have to be paid and the amount of tax could be calculated over 5 or 10 years. (To learn more about this strategy, call the IRS and ask for Form 4972 and Form 1040. You can request both by calling 1-800-TAX-FORM.) Table 14-1 from The AARP Investment Program shows (1) how taxes could affect the growth of a lump-sum distribution if the taxes were paid on it using 10-year averaging (that means the tax is calculated using a 10-year period) with 20 percent of the distribution withheld at the time it is paid out and (2) how that money would grow if transferred into an IRA.

The Rule of 72: Both Sides

The Rule of 72 is an easy way for all investors to find out two important pieces of investment data: (1) how long it will take for money to double when it's invested at a fixed interest rate, and (2) how long it will take for money to lose half its purchasing value.

"The Rule of 72 is a two-sided coin," says Frazier Wellmeier, a certified financial planner at Smith Barney in West Palm Beach, Florida. "And investors need to understand both sides of it to create an investment plan that will work out for them."

Table 14-1. How Taxes Affect the Growth of Lump-Sum Distribution (Using 10-Year Averaging)

	Special averaging: pay taxes now	An IRA transfer: pay taxes later
Distribution amount	$80,000	$80,000
Current taxes (using 1986 tax rates)	$11,110	$0
After-tax amount, or what's left to invest after taxes	$68,890	$80,000
Rate of return	7%	7%
Number of years invested	10 years	10 years
Tax bracket	28%	0%
Growth of money over 10 years	$112,643 (after taxes)	$157,372 (before taxes, which will be due upon distribution.)

SOURCE: The AARP Investment Program from Scudder.

Here's how to use the Rule of 72: To find out how long it will take for your investment dollars to double, when invested at a specified rate, simply divide 72 by that rate of return. For example, if you have $1000 invested into something earning 6 percent each year, 72 divided by 6 equals 12. Which means, if $1000 remains continually invested in something yielding 6 percent per year, compounding and growing each year, in a dozen years that $1000 will then have grown in value to $2000. (72 divided by 6 is 12).

To find out how long it will take for your money to lose half its value, look at the Rule of 72 from its other side.

"Let's say that the inflation rate is 5 percent," says Robert Glovsky, host of *The Money Experts* on WHDH radio in Boston and director at Tofias, Fleishmann & Shapiro. "Five into 72 equals 14.4. What that says is a dollar today will be worth 50 cents in 14.4 years if we have 5 percent inflation. Or another way to phrase it is, if you have a dollar today, in 14.5 years you'll need 2 dollars to buy what that one does right now."

To use the Rule of 72 for your retirement planning, use both sides of it: one side to see how long it will take for money to grow, the other to gauge how the earnings from your investments measure up against rates of inflation.

"I don't have discretionary income to invest for the future," says Bill Blackwell, an automobile dealer in North Palm Beach, Florida. "Every time I turn around my overhead gets higher and higher. And the little money I can put aside goes into savings." Blackwell, the father of two, is caught in the "there's always something" syndrome. Like many thirty-something parents, he plans on investing "later on" for his own retirement.

Right now he's on the pay-as-you-go plan. So moving his money from a savings account where he can get his hands on it immediately and into the investment arena, isn't a top priority for him.

But even people with discretionary money to invest aren't always inflation-conscious investors.

"Retirees often face a big problem," adds Glovsky. "People in that age group have to think in terms of longevity and how inflation will impact their investments."

Glovsky explained that if someone age 65 had half a million dollars, needed $50,000 to live on comfortably annually, and decided to invest all her money into 20-year bonds paying 7 percent, she would have an income from that investment of $35,000. Add that income to his estimate of roughly $15,000 in Social Security benefits, and Glovsky said that individual would have the annual income desired.

"But," he adds, "If inflation is at 5 percent, in the next year that person will need $52,500 just to break even. And they won't have that extra money because they have developed an investment portfolio with no ability to plan for inflation."

While pure bond investing has provided bondholders with a steady income stream, investing in bonds doesn't always keep up with inflation. The story for stocks is a different one.

History shows that investing in the stock market is one way to fight, if not beat, inflation. Over the 10 years from December 1983 through December 1992, the Consumer Price Index (which measures the changes in prices and is one indicator of the inflation rate) has been as high as 6.10 percent; as low as 1.10 percent; and has averaged 3.82 percent. Compare that to the compounded average annual return on the S&P 500, with dividends reinvested, of 16.2 percent, and it's easy to see why so many people say stocks provide an inflation edge.

For people in the planning stage for their retirement, investing in both bonds, for the fixed rate of return and steady income, and stocks, for their growth potential, often makes good sense.

"Using the Rule of 72 to figure out how far your dollars will go is one of the most important things you can do in your life," adds Wellmeier. "Inflation affects us for the rest of our lives and if we're not careful, we could run out of income before we run out of breath."

Some Nest-Egg-Building Ideas—Taking Inflation into Account

What sized nest egg do you have to have if you'd like to draw $2000 a month from it for, say, 25 years? That's what I wanted to know. To find out I asked Derek Sasveld, a financial analyst at Ibbotson Associates (financial number crunching specialists in Chicago).

Calculations to the following "How-much-do-I-need-if . . . ?" questions are based upon the following assumptions: First, that the total nest egg amount produced at age 65 is always working and at age 65 is invested in products earning either 5 or 10 percent each year; second, that at age 90 the nest egg is depleted—as in, there's no money left in it to pass on, period; and finally, the future value of the $2000 a month income that the nest egg provides, assumes a 3 percent annual rate of inflation.

1. You're 25 years old today, plan on retiring in 40 years at age 65 and dying 25 years later at age 90, and want to build a nest egg from which you would not only invest but could also take out (in today's dollars) $2000 a month for 25 years.

a. How big would that nest egg have to be at age 65?

b. How much money per month would you have to begin investing at age 25 to be able to acquire that sized nest egg?

c. What would a one-lump-sum investment have to be at age 25 to make that nest egg possible?

d. At a 3 percent rate of inflation, you can expect the cost of living to double every_____years, which means by 2035, you'll need_____to buy what $10 does today.

Answers:

a. $1,552,623.26 (*invested at 5%*), $957,955.59 (*at 10%*)

b. $1,043.03 (*at 5%*), $168.49 (*at 10%*)

c. $220,543.43 (*at 5%*), $21,165.96 (*at 10%*)

d. 23.5 years, $32.62

2. Suppose you were 35 years old, had 30 years to retirement, expected to live to age 90, and wanted to build a nest egg from which you would not only invest but could take out (in today's dollars) $2000 a month for 25 years.

a. How big would that nest egg have to be at age 65?

b. How much money per month would you have to begin investing at age 35 to acquire that nest egg amount?

c. What would a one-lump-sum investment have to be at age 35 to make that sized nest egg possible?

d. At a 3 percent rate of inflation, you can expect the cost of living to double every_____years, which means by 2025, you'll need_____to buy what $10 does today.

Answers:

a. $1,155,297.51 (*invested at 5%*), $712,808.96 (*at 10%*)

b. $1,411.14 (*at 5%*), $342.81 (*at 10%*)

c. $267,309.79 (*at 5%*), $40,850.05 (*at 10%*)

d. 23.5 years, $24.27

3. Suppose you were 45 years old, had 20 years to retirement, expected to live to age 90, and wanted to build a nest egg from which you would not only invest but could also take out (in today's dollars) $2000 a month for 25 years.

a. How big would that nest egg have to be at age 65?

b. How much money per month would you have to begin investing at age 45 to acquire that nest egg amount?

c. What would a one-lump-sum investment at age 45 have to be to make that nest egg possible?

d. At a 3 percent rate of inflation, you can expect the cost of living to double every_____years, which means by 2015, you'll need_____to buy what $10 does today.

Answers:
a. $859,649.86 (*invested at 5%*), $530,396.84 (*at 10%*)
b. $2,109.79 (*at 5%*), $732.61 (*at 10%*)
c. $323,992.99 (*at 5%*), $78,840.11 (*at 10%*)
d. 23.5 years, $18.06

4. Suppose you were 55 years old, had 10 years to retirement, expected to live to age 90, and wanted to build a nest egg from which you would not only invest but could also take out (in today's dollars) $2000 a month for 25 years.
   a. How big would that nest egg have to be at age 65?
   b. How much money per month would you have to begin investing at age 55 to acquire that nest egg amount?
   c. What would a one-lump-sum investment at age 55 have to be to make that nest egg possible?
   d. At a 3 percent rate of inflation, you can expect the cost of living to double every_____years, which means by 2005, you'll need_____to buy what $10 does today.

Answers:
a. $639,660.23 (*invested at 5%*), $394,665.07 (*at 10%*)
b. $4,127.05 (*at 5%*), $1, 959.05 (*at 10%*)
c. $392,695.89 (*at 5%*), $152,160.47 (*at 10%*)
d. 23.5 years, $13.44

5. Suppose you were 65 years old today, thinking about retiring right now, then living until age 90.
   a. How big would that nest egg have to be to be able to take $2000 a month from it?
   b. At a 3 percent rate of inflation, you can expect the cost of living to double every_____years, which means by 2020, you'll need_____to buy what $10 does today.

Answers:
a. $475,967.28 (*invested at 5%*), $293,667.88 (*at 10%*)
b. 23.5 years, 20.94

15

Getting the Help You Need

Getting Help from a Financial Planner or Advisor

Financial planners and financial advisors can provide a great service to those who want help in developing their long-term retirement plans.

While the words *financial planner* often get used as sort of a blanket term covering a host of professional advice givers, including everyone from brokers and insurance agents to attorneys and accountants, there are actually certified financial planners, CFPs, who have earned that accreditation.

While letters of accreditation and skills don't always go hand in hand, looking at the letters behind a financial advice giver's name will provide you with a clue as to the amount of education that person has acquired. Finding out how well that person does his or her job, however, means digging a little deeper.

Here are some suggestions on how to whittle down the world of financial advisor choices to a manageable list:

- Ask for references. Word-of-mouth recommendations from someone you respect is a great way to start interviewing financial advisors.

- Check credentials. Every financial advisor who is charging a fee and offering investment advice is required to be registered by the Securities and Exchange Commission and by the state in which he or she resides. Registered representatives selling securities must also be licensed with the National Association of Securities Dealers (NASD). And anyone selling insurance products is required to hold insurance licenses granted by the appropriate insurance authorities.

To check a registered representative's track record regarding customer complaints, you may call the NASD at 1-800-289-9999.

- Using the names of the advisors referred by friends, along with any other financial sources found on your own, begin setting up appointments in which you "interview" potential financial advisors. Because it's *your* financial future on the line, finding an individual that is competent and with whom you'd like to work may take an interview or two. But the time spent will be well worth it.

- Prepare for the interviews. Have a list of questions prepared and make sure some of them include asking about that person's financial education, licenses, and accreditation; her or his employment history; and the client list. Try asking that person how he or she would invest a specific lump sum of money. Good financial advisors won't make any recommendations before understanding your whole financial situation and discussing your risk tolerance and long-term financial needs.

- Ask about compensation. Basically there are three ways that financial planners and advisors get paid. There are those who sell their advice and information for a fee, often hourly; those who give or sell advice in conjunction with financial products and then receive a commission for the products they sell; and those who play both fields—charging a combination of fees and receiving commissions.

  Finding out which method of payment the financial advisor you select uses is not only important for you to learn, but it's a question advisors expect to be asked.

- Think long-term. The relationship that develops between you and your financial planner or advice giver may last a lifetime. And it's one that often winds up being a personal as well as a professional one. Because of the financial intimacy of the relationship, make sure the advisor you select is not only one you can trust, but is also someone you are comfortable working with.

Even though each of us has some level of money management skills, in our rapidly changing world we all need continual financial education no matter what our age or investment experience. After all, experts on Wall Street get advice and counsel on where and how to invest money every day of the week. Why shouldn't we?

If you'd like more information on retirement planning, there are many respectable resources out there. The ones I'm most familiar with are from mutual fund families. One is T. Rowe Price's *Retirees' Workbook,* which can be obtained, free, by calling 1-800-638-7890. There are two parts to this fund family's retirement guide, and it's quite possibly the best free workbook that you'll find on the subject. Not only do the workbooks speak to the issues facing retirees—such as cash-flows and inflation—but each is chock full of information, charts, and guidelines to help you map your retirement plans.

Another resource is any of the retirement literature available through The AARP Investment Program from Scudder. To obtain their free retirement literature, call 1-800-233-2277. Or those from Fidelity Investments can be gotten by calling 1-800-544-4774. The Oppenheimer Fund family also has a host of retirement guides. Contact them at 1-800-525-7048.

Getting Help On-Line

Anyone with a computer can really have the upper hand when it comes to creating a long-term retirement plan for him- or herself.

For under $20, you can buy some terrific software programs, install them on your own personal computers, and then spend literally hours playing around with different investment product choices, creating a variety of long-term savings plans that could work for you.

One that I've had fun with is Vanguard's Retirement Planner. The cost is $17.50 and worth every penny of it. The color graphics in the program make what might otherwise be a dull chore—retirement planning—into an interesting game.

What I like about Vanguard's Retirement Planner is how easy it is to work. Not only can you create a bunch of different long-term investment plan scenarios, the program lets you look back at historical performance of different investment products, look ahead at how any kind of retirement scheme you come up with might work, and look at whether your current retirement plans are surefooted enough to carry you through your retirement years.

There are two downsides to this program: (1) the program is not available for Macintosh or Apple users, just for IBM-PCs and their clones; and (2) you've got to have a color monitor to be able to take full advantage of all the things the program can do. Other than that, it's a beauty.

Business Week magazine offered this alphabetical listing of retirement planning software in their May 23, 1994, issue:

Program	Cost	Phone	Comments
Fidelity Retirement Planner	$15	800-457-1768	More an educational tool—teaching the value of saving early—than a budgeting and asset management program.
Price Waterhouse Retirement Planning	$45	800-752-6234	Allows you to alter savings and income rates during working years and retirement. Also offers a $19 "lite" version.
Retire ASAP	$99	800-225-8246	The only program that permits calculations for situations where partner isn't a spouse. Atari version available.
Rich & Retired	$66	800-556-7526	Most comprehensive program; line-item-budgeting feature allows user to see where to cut expenses.
T. Rowe Price Retirement Planning Kit	$15	800-541-1472	Shows benefits of periodic withdrawal vs. one-time withdrawal. Beware of sales pitch: recommends T. Rowe Price funds.
Vanguard Retirement Planner	$17.50	800-876-1840	Strong graphics make it easy to use. Uses sliding thermometer bar to show effect of changing variables on income.
Wealthbuilder	$70	800-346-2024	Financial planning program, with strong portfolio management capabilities. Access to on-line data.

16

What the Pros Suggest

When I invited five of my stockbroker and financial advisor friends to join me for a round-table discussion about investing for retirement, my goal was to learn how people in the different decades of their working lives could accumulate wealth through long-term investing. Much to my surprise, however, that luncheon yielded more than just investment ideas.

Along with some diversified retirement investment strategies, these securities pros also brought to the table insights on retirement investing and stories about how their clients had actually invested at different stages in their lives.

If there was one thing that underscored this luncheon discussion, it wasn't whether or not this handful of financial experts agreed with one another regarding retirement investment suggestions, it was how tuned in each one was with understanding the financial reality that we all are different. Because of this fact, when it comes to investing for our own retirements, there are no answers to questions about how much money we need to invest or which products to choose that are right for everybody. But there is one rule anyone can follow: Start saving early.

What follows is the round-table discussion. (The names of the brokers have been changed and the firms they work for purposely have not been given. I'm "Dian" the moderator.

> DIAN: If you're in your twenties and have some money to invest for retirement, what would your investment suggestions be?

PETER: I'd be aggressive. Very aggressive. And invest in things like growth stocks or stock mutual funds like growth, or aggressive growth, funds.

DIAN: Any ideas to young people about how to get the money to buy stocks or mutual funds?

MICHAEL: They've got to learn to pay themselves first. And get into the habit of taking a percentage out of every paycheck they bring home so that they can start to save that money. Then later they should invest it.

PETER: Some of the money they receive is going to be gift money, too. Like from their parents or grandparents.

NANCY: And from wedding gifts.

BILL: Back to Michael's point of "pay yourself first," for some people that might mean saving fifty dollars a month until they get to maybe one thousand or two thousand dollars. With those larger amounts of money there are more choices about where to invest. Unfortunately, there's no one right place to invest, because everyone is different.

DIAN: So if we are to try and think about the average working person, who may or may not have a college degree and is in their early twenties, what ought they be doing to plan for their retirement?

PETER: Some of their money should be in an IRA and a 401(k). But the twenty-year-olds that I know are saving their money for a car, a home, a stereo, or whatever.

BILL: You have to really understand the mindset of someone in their twenties. To get them to have to put away money for their IRA so they can get at it at age fifty-nine and a half is a very, very difficult concept to grasp.

DIAN: I know. But even if it's a hard notion to get across, they have to make choices as to what they do with their money.

NANCY: Well, the most important choice is to start saving.

PETER: That's right. And then the discipline is to put your money into an IRA or a 401(k)—and to get into that habit when you're young.

DIAN: What about a plain old savings account?

NANCY: Everybody needs to have liquid assets. Opening a savings account—or putting your money into a money-market mutual fund— is vital to taking care of life's everyday financial surprises. So savings accounts are something everybody ought to strive to have. Always.

PETER: The problem there is that that money is not always really earmarked for retirement and could be spent in other places. But Nancy's right, you need to be able to get your hands on cash when you need it.

MARK: I have a twenty-three-year-old son who understands the pitfalls and advantages of investing into mutual funds and variable annuities. He and his friends have money taken out of their paychecks and they know the money is not meant to be touched until they are age fifty-nine and a half.

These kids are greedy, they are hungry, they want to accumulate wealth, they love the fact that there is a guaranteed death benefit on these annuities because they feel they can be as aggressive as they want to be in life. And, if they get married, their beneficiaries will be taken care of. Plus they also like the fact that, in an annuity, there is some insulation against legal judgments—should anything ever happen to them because they're young and reckless.

But these kids are a lot more sophisticated than I ever was at age twenty-three. No question about it. And they have fifty or seventy-five dollars a month taken out of their checking account and added to their tax-deferred variable annuities . . . even understanding penalties!

PETER: But these kids aren't common. They had you as a dad.

MARK: Well, I don't know about that. All I know is there are some high school kids that might not know Chaucer but are very money-savvy.

MICHAEL: My twenty-one-year-old daughter has an IRA with money in it invested into an aggressive growth fund. But I agree; it's not the normal behavior.

BILL: Everybody I see is different. Take, for instance, the twenty-three-year-old who is self-employed and runs his own plumbing service versus the twenty-three-year-old who works for a corporation and has the benefit of a salary reduction or 401(k) plan. To each, I would give completely different advice. Both would need to have savings and investment direction, but the self-employed businessperson is going to need more capital at hand just to keep his business afloat than the corporate employee does.

NANCY: Something that I do for my clients is to suggest to them that as parents and grandparents they should, rather than giving money to their kids, make some investments for them.

It seems to be easier once a young person owns something, like a stock or mutual fund or insurance product, to get him or her into investing because he or she is more familiar with it. And these kids like to read about the investments they have. Plus they have a tendency to watch the financial news.

So what happens is, most of my clients that have gifted investments to their children or grandchildren, have kids who wind up becoming investors on their own. One of the great lessons that a parent can show their kids is how to save and invest.

MARK: But how do we explain to the children of our parent's generation that you can be so conservative that you're really in danger of investing in too-conservative investments? Such as CDs?

MICHAEL: I get a lot of people who say OK, I'm in the 401(k) at my firm and this is my allocation. And then they either have all or a vast majority of this retirement money in a GIC or a fixed-income product.

MARK: Or in low-grade corporate bonds because they've heard that bonds are "safe."

BILL: At my brokerage firm, they did a study of where our employees had invested their 401(k)s. At that time we had a choice of ten different mutual funds to invest into. And of the support staff that participated in the study, they found that 80 percent of them had their retirement savings in money-market accounts.

Those results show that even in our business, even as professionals, so much knowledge tends to get overlooked. And we don't realize that often the average investor doesn't really have a clue as to what to do with his money.

Which is why I would include zero-coupon Treasury bonds in the category for how twenty-year-olds can start to acquire wealth for their retirement or savings accounts. Even though we all would probably agree that the best inflation fighter over the long haul is the stock market.

But, for the average twenty-three or twenty-four-year old, and let's assume his or her parents never owned stocks, even if some of the purchasing power of these zeros may be eaten away or eroded as the years go by, if you've gotten that young person to invest in a growth fund and the value of it is down, you might not ever get them to invest in the stock market again. So zeros provide a nice introduction into long-term investing.

NANCY: I think you've made a good point in that we tend to overlook things ourselves. One of the first things young people—and all of us—need to do is to educate ourselves to what "inflation" and "nominal rates of return" mean. As well as on the prospects of being able to live on Social Security.

BILL: I think we tend to get way ahead of ourselves when it comes to recommending to twenty-year-olds where to invest their IRA money.

While we all may think that an aggressive growth fund might be best for them, they might not understand how stock prices, and the net asset value of mutual funds, can jump around. Maybe some need to get their feet wet by investing in a blue-chip stock or stock fund. Or again in Treasury zeros.

MARK: And then warn them to "beware of investing tips" that they hear from their buddies.

PETER: Well, I'm all for people using funds.

DIAN: If you have one thousand dollars to invest, you can really invest into four different funds and create your own portfolio of funds.

MARK: That's true. But I just don't know why anyone would want to generate a 1099 unless they had to. So we use variable annuities like American Skandia, Fortis, and Sun America which give people a choice of load or no-load funds to choose from. I think these nonqualified tax-deferred variable annuities are one of the great concepts for folks who don't want a 1099 form. This is, of course, in addition to whatever qualified retirement plan they may be in.

DIAN: Let's go to age thirty. If it were a perfect world, would you still have people investing ideally in aggressive funds?

MARK: So much depends upon when these people get married—if they get married—and when they decide to start a family.

A lot of people I know are buying their first home in their early thir-

ties, if they really got off to a good start. And at age thirty-six and thirty-eight, after selling that first home—quite often for a nice hunk of
change—they would like to have some cash for when Johnny goes into
college. So, I'm going to start to use some zero-coupon bonds for the
people who are in their thirties and have kids say eight, nine, ten, and
eleven years old.

DIAN: What about a universal life policy?

MARK: No whole or universal life insurance. I would use term insurance. I
believe in term insurance—period. And let your investments be your
investments.

DIAN: I can't believe everybody agrees on that. I can just imagine how the
insurance people will respond to that. There are things that you can do
with insurance products you can't do with other investments. After all,
at the time of death, insurance contracts offer some attractive benefits.

PETER: I'm using very little fixed income and no zeros at all now.

DIAN: Why?

PETER: Under the present level of interest rates, I just don't see the merit of
locking into these rates for the long haul. I wouldn't sell anybody zeros
that were to mature in twenty or thirty years from now.

MICHAEL: That would be suicide.

PETER: With inflation and everything, I just can't do it.

NANCY: Well, I have coupled zeros with aggressive products to a limited
degree. Not to guarantee that they (the zeros) are going to double or
triple in value, but to guarantee that even if the stock market plunged
downward, they still would have their original investment back when
the zeros matured.

MICHAEL: Some of the mutual funds do that, too.

BILL: Just to smooth out the returns, zeros can be good. We all know that
there are going to be good years and bad years in the market. And
again, you don't want to turn somebody who is in their twenties off to
the stock market. After the biggest bull market in history the market
could go through a few years where there are tough times for aggressive funds.

DIAN: I talked with someone earlier this week who said that they would
never even think of investing their retirement money into something
that could lose money. This person is a flat-out bond investor. Period.
His retirement plan investment strategy was to invest into a combination of zero-coupon Treasury bonds and to create a laddered portfolio
of Treasury bonds maturing out not longer than seven years. "I don't
ever want to lose my money," is what he said.

MARK: So what if inflation is 6 percent and his average total returns on all
these investments is 4.3 percent? He does not view that as losing
money?

DIAN: No, he doesn't. His big concern was keeping his money intact and
not losing any of it. He wasn't concerned about inflation or the loss of

future buying power. I don't think most people understand what those buying-power concepts are really all about.

BILL: By allocating a certain amount to fixed income, you can dollar cost average each year into zeros and wind up building quite a nice portfolio—with a large bit of money coming due at retirement.

But people tend to focus on the value of their investments today. It's very difficult to get them to look out over the long-term. And when it comes down to the aggressive funds, they are going to zigzag in value.

DIAN: And bonds, if held until they mature, won't lose value. They just might not have the buying power you hoped they would.

OK, let's move into the forties. That's when all the experts say that you're supposed to have more money, that is, disposable cash, available to you. Think that's so?

PETER: No. That's the time when you go through divorce.

MARK: The forties should be the age of covered call writing. [Covered call writing is an investment strategy in which shares of stocks you own are used in an option-writing contract.]

If someone has been successful and they have worked for Wal-Mart, Sears, Procter and Gamble, or Ford, their knowledge of equities becomes "Oh yeah, I have stocks. I have thirteen hundred shares of Sears because I work there."

Once people are comfortable with the stocks they own, and the portfolios they've built, they would be wise to listen to the concept of covered call writing.

NANCY: People in their forties are also much more tax-conscious then they were when they were younger because they are usually earning more than ever before, too.

MARK: If people have limited experience in the market and big holdings in one or two companies, covered calls can work out well.

PETER: I don't recommend that to my people. It's too difficult a concept for many to understand.

NANCY: I do. But I've never had a hard time explaining it. I say it's like buying a house and then renting it out: If the house goes up dramatically in value, you give up some of your upside and have to sell the stock. But, you've collected rent on it all the time. If the stock goes down in value, you get to keep the rent and never sell the house, that is, the stock.

MARK: Once covered call writing is explained and people start to see the premium money coming in, they love it. Otherwise, what often happens is that shares of the stock are kept in a vault. And if that stock is going down in value, they are doing nothing about it, plus they are losing an investment opportunity.

MICHAEL: How about international investing?

PETER: I like to suggest it.

BILL: I see that as synonymous with aggressive investments.

MARK: I really don't feel that international investing is prudent for these people. . . . And an investment that trades in another currency is adding what I feel is an undue currency exposure for our investors.

If my clients want to invest internationally, I talk to them about companies like Heinz or Archer Daniels. These companies do business all over the world. And there is no currency risk involved when investing in them.

DIAN: You're not going to suggest international or global investing, Mark?

MARK: We are very selective when it comes to investing internationally and prefer to suggest stocks of A-rated companies. I did some asset allocation shifts recently suggesting today's investors have less than 10 percent of their assets in global companies. . . . But I'm happier with companies like US West, which has money in Czechoslovakia and Hungary, over funds.

BILL: I think that I'd be doing my clients a disservice if I didn't suggest that some of their assets be invested overseas—given that, in the past fifty years, the greatest returns have come from stocks of companies outside of the United States.

For someone with a modest net worth, 10 percent of their assets into a good global fund can make sense. But you don't put a conservative investor in something like a single-country fund.

DIAN: When do you start to see people really concerned about retirement? In their forties or fifties?

PETER: I would say it's in both decades.

DIAN: Don't you think that in the forties it's a real kick-off time again for very aggressive investments?

PETER: I do, personally.

BILL: So do I.

MICHAEL: It all depends upon the person's lifestyle. If they got married young and had their children young, most forty-year-olds that I know are now just getting married for the second time.

MARK: I was going to say that, too. Many are on their second or third families.

BILL: For people in their forties or fifties, I start reminding them that the possibility is greater now than not that they will live in retirement as long as they have worked!

So, they need to get a portion of their money into stocks, stock funds, or a covered call writing program.

And it's also a time when parents of these forty- and fifty-year-olds are starting to gift their kids—these adults—money.

MICHAEL: There are also a lot of forty-year-olds in that sandwiched situation—they've got kids of their own at home plus they have to take care of their own aging parents. And putting money away for the long run is difficult.

PETER: Yes, but the first long-term dollar you invest should go into that IRA or 401(k). In other words, lock up the money so that you aren't able to blow it.

DIAN: In all the years, collectively, in which you've been doing IRAs, how much have fees eaten up the yields on these things?

MARK: We hear horror stories all the time about people who have diversified between seven or eight different mutual funds and have really been clobbered by fees. I'm not talking of the sales load, but of the annual ongoing fees for maintaining those accounts. And I see people in their forties who come in and say that they have three CDs in their bank IRAs and two different funds. To these people I suggest putting everything into one account.

BILL: Diversity among trustees is how fees can get to be a problem.

PETER: On fees, I look at it like this: If a client has an IRA in which they did a lot of trading in stocks, the costs can really add up. It's 2 percent to buy, 2 percent to sell . . . and then you buy another stock. And then another.

Whereas, if you had taken the original ten thousand dollars you used to buy a stock, and bought say Templeton Growth fund and decided to switch from that fund into another in the family at some point, you'd never have to pay another fee.

When it comes to retirement planning, younger people are more equity-oriented. So, if you're in the right fund family, an individual can start in an equity fund, move into bond funds, say in their forties and fifties, and then switch into a balanced fund in their sixties. Funds are much more cost-effective.

DIAN: So in the fifties are people supposed to stay aggressively invested?

PETER: I might be more conservative on the equity side here.

BILL: Instead of growth funds you could move into blue chips that pay dividends.

PETER: Or balanced funds.

MARK: Insurance. You start getting inquiries about second survivorship life. Or "second to die." People are seeing what their parents are paying in premiums—because their parents are living longer and many have health problems. So in the fifties is when I see many starting to ask estate planning questions.

Plus, who doesn't know someone who dropped dead at thirty-eight or forty?

And, since statistics say that people are something like three or four times more likely to be disabled than drop dead in midlife, folks who have never thought about disability insurance in their twenties, thirties, and forties, who now have got eight, ten, and twelve years to go to retirement, begin to ask about disability income coverage.

So the fifties are when some insurance and estate planning often begins.

MICHAEL: Variable annuities really can make sense at this stage of the game. If you're lucky, you're only nine years away from retirement. And if you've got money to invest in variable annuities, it will grow and compound tax-deferred until you need it.

NANCY: At this age we start to plug our clients into programs that will show them exactly how much money they'll need to have to be able to live on.

DIAN: So it sounds like by the time someone gets into their fifties, retirement is *real.*

EVERYONE: *Yes!*

DIAN: And up until then, the retirement attitude is sort of a "yeah, yeah, yeah, I've got better things to do with my money"?

MARK: Or they could be starting a new career.

MICHAEL: Or IBM lays them off and they've got to find something else to do.

DIAN: OK, let's go to the sixties. Are people thinking about their money, or Social Security's?

MICHAEL: Well, right now many studies show that they will need 70 percent of their preretirement income to maintain their current standard of living.

PETER: Let me throw a wrinkle in here. You have two sorts of people: the ones who start to take either all the money out, or use cashflow distributions. And then you have the people who say that they're never going to need the money. So they just throw it into an estate. Obviously you're going to treat each case differently.

MARK: Unless they are destitute and need the income, sixty-year-olds are focusing on seventy and a half. So the first thing that I would say about what are the real identifiable signs of people in their sixties is that a lot of them are looking at seventy and a half. And they are not touching a penny of their savings. Unless the government requires them to.

PETER: That's right. People aren't going to spend any of their nest egg unless they really need it.

BILL: Lots of people in their twenties, thirties, forties, fifties, and sixties have only put their money in the bank. And it's often that we get the call from someone around fifty years old who realizes that there is no way his or her CD money is going to get him through retirement.

We tend to forget that roughly 90 percent of Americans' liquid net worth is still in banks.

MICHAEL: People didn't complain in the nineteen eighties when interest rates were roughly 15 percent and inflation was running at 12 percent. By the time taxes were paid, usually their money had lost buying power. But most people didn't realize that.

NANCY: We talked earlier about the variable annuity. I've had some clients in their sixties purchase immediate annuities. That way they are guaranteed that they are going to have a certain income stream—no matter what happens to them—for life.

MICHAEL: The sixties are a real good time for people to start investing in tax-free bonds.

DIAN: Are you sure? They still have the seventies and eighties to live through.

MICHAEL: They are going to be pulling money out of retirement accounts, and if they live in a state like New York, New Jersey, or California, it generally makes sense for them to have munis. They don't have to be long-term ones.

That's what I often hear, anyway. People don't want Uncle Sam to get a hold of any more of their money than is absolutely necessary. These people have worked all their lives for their retirement monies and when they retire, they realize that the money has to last a long time.

PETER: I've found that even though clients may realize that they have an inflation problem, they still need to have some exposure to equities.

I've also found that the mentality of this sixty-something age group is one that says, "OK. I've accumulated this nest egg and I want to make sure it doesn't disappear. But now that I'm going to retire, I don't want to hassle with equities now."

So, even though they may know about inflation and its risks on eating up their principal, most prefer the fixed-income products.

BILL: What I hear from some wealthy retirees is "I want to spend my kids' inheritance." One says his kid is a doctor and doesn't need any money, another says his son married the wrong girl, and together they agree that "I'm not giving my kids a dime."

Then I get the other people who live a very modest lifestyle because they want to leave something to their kids.

DIAN: Yeah, people seem to be all over the board on what to leave to their kids.

PETER: Many are taking care of themselves first.

MICHAEL: And how many times have you heard a disgruntled retiree say about his kids that a canceled check is not a "thank you"?

DIAN: Let's add age seventy.

MARK: The seventies is the age of Social Security. But now you have a best seller on your hands.

Carnegie Mellon did a study on how long Social Security will survive. If the Social Security trust does not implement everything that we've been talking about—such as investing differently as the times and needs change—there won't be much, if any, money in Social Security by the time we get to age seventy.

So the fact is, the same discipline that we were talking about, by using equities and managing Social Security the way you would manage your corporate pension account, makes good sense.

If the government doesn't implement that kind of investment strategy, your readers could have a real big surprise when they get to their seventies.

What was the figure this week . . . that Social Security would run out by 2032?

MICHAEL: I recently read where the funds for Medicare could be gone by 2005 or 6. That's about ten years from now.

MARK: So one of the prefaces to your book might be: This isn't just a guide for the individual, this is a blueprint for the government. Unless diversified, prudent, investment-grade instruments are utilized—outside of just government bonds—some of these readers may not be getting anything from Social Security in the decades to come.

PETER: The key to all retirement planning is diversification. Diversification is a safety net.

NANCY: That's right. We all know how risky investing into just one investment product can be.

MARK: Many people in their seventies have also sold their bigger homes and now are living in smaller places.

NANCY: And they've sold their businesses.

PETER: Some aren't necessarily driving the fancy cars any more. Or taking fancy vacations.

DIAN: And I see people in their seventies who are spending their money like it's going out of style.

PETER: That's true, too. Then there are others who decide they just want to sit home and do nothing. Or are ill and can't do anything but stay confined.

BILL: I wonder how these answers might differ if you had a round-table discussion with brokers from Kansas City, Missouri, versus those of us in South Florida?

If you're coming from the Rust Belt, brokers there are much more equity-focused.

MARK: But people everywhere read the same magazines and watch *Wall Street Week.*

NANCY: Oh . . . don't forget systematic withdrawals. In the seventies is when people have to start taking their money out of their IRAs and Keoghs and investing into mutual funds. Then using systematic withdrawal plans is a great way to have some income and invest, too. But what I've found is that people don't really radically change their investment style decade to decade. If they are conservative investors to begin with, they seem to stay that way.

MARK: But there are some trends regarding the amounts of money they have to invest and when they get that money. For instance, real estate. In their sixties and seventies many times people invest again in real estate—like in a small second home or condo, because of the tax laws. If they are lucky enough to take advantage and use a second home as a write-off, you've got seventy-two-year-olds looking for townhouses as an extra investment or as a vacation place to live.

So you'd have to say real estate is back in their retirement planning.

DIAN: Let's move on to the last question: How much money do you think you have to have accumulated—in today's dollars—by age seventy to be able to live a comfortable life?

MARK: For which lifestyle? To live in Joplin, Missouri, or Palm Beach, Florida?

DIAN: To live in MO.

MICHAEL: Well, it depends upon whether you're going to deplete the principal or not and what your lifestyle is like.

MARK: There is no set number. But many people today, feel that they could live a comfortable retirement on thirty-six to forty thousand dollars a year. That's in today's dollar terms.

PETER: I knew of a man who retired at forty-nine on seven hundred and fifty thousand dollars. I didn't think that would be enough for this man to stay retired on and figured that one day he'd have to go back to work. Which he recently did.

DIAN: How about a nest egg of six hundred thousand dollars? Could that be a reasonable amount to shoot for?

Drawing down from that, if you were sixty-five years old—and the money was still earning 7 percent annually—that amount would bring you in about thirty-nine thousand a year for the next thirty years.

That means if I were sixty-five today, my six-hundred-thousand-dollar nest egg would bring me thirty-nine thousand dollars a year until I was ninety-five. At which time it, and maybe even me, would be depleted.

PETER: But that doesn't factor in inflation.

DIAN: No it doesn't. But people have to have a goal—an amount of money that they try to attain.

PETER: It might be alright for some. But not for everyone.

MARK: There's one thing we've forgotten. Cash.

I think that there are an awful lot of people in their seventies and eighties in this country who are hoarding cash. I mean literally, with the boxes under the bed with gold coins in them.

I have a client who can't pass by a coin store without going in and buying. He believes in having gold on hand. Along with cash.

MICHAEL: That's like the old bearer bonds people used to keep in their bank vaults.

People like to have money available to them that no one else knows anything about. Which brings us to the bottom line: For most people, all this financial planning business is very individual and private stuff.

DIAN: That's true—and quite frankly, says it all. So if there is one thing that you would advise anyone who is thinking about saving money for their retirement do today, what would that be?

EVERYONE: Start saving *now*.

17

Investing throughout Your Lifetime

You've got to plant the apple tree if you want to get the apples.

FRAZIER WELLMEIER,
CERTIFIED FINANCIAL PLANNER

No two of us are exactly alike. Each of us has a uniquely different set of life's circumstances that we are facing, financial incomes that we live with, hopes and dreams like no one ever before us. Consequently, managing our lives along with our finances is a challenge that is ours and ours alone.

This chapter is broken down into six decade segments, beginning with The Twenties and ending with The Seventies. Each decade segment begins with the profile of an individual or couple whose age falls within that decade and highlights what their retirement plans have been. That's followed by a checklist of guidelines to follow that will help you create your own retirement portfolio.

Before we look at the kinds of moves to take to ensure some financial freedom and security for yourself and your loved ones during your mature years, it's important to underline, once again, why investing a portion of your long-term retirement money is so important. In a word—a word that has come up again and again in these pages—the reason is: inflation.

If there were no such thing as inflation and prices were fixed, never changing, instead of investing for our retirement all we'd have to do is save our money. Collect it. And keep collecting it so that we'd have buckets full to spend over our lifetimes. Unfortunately, money that is just collected isn't earning any interest or compounding for us. Consequently, while on the one hand we might be accumulating money, on the other that money isn't working for us. And we need our money to work for us because prices on goods and services over time tend to increase thanks to inflation. Every time I walk into a store at the mall, visit the grocery store, or ask vendors at a crafts fair how much they're selling their handmade jewelry for, I'm reminded of that fact.

So investing money for retirement is as much about collecting money as it is making it grow. If we don't allow our money to grow, creating a golden nest egg—one that will allow us to keep our current lifestyles intact—becomes all the more difficult. We are, after all, not saving and investing to be poorer financially in our older years, but to maintain our current lifestyle and perhaps even be richer.

Don't Forget the Rule of 72 . . .

Remember the Rule of 72 from Chapter 14? As was pointed out earlier, not only can that simple little formula show how many years it will take for your money to double at a specified rate, it can also be used to show how much buying power your money will have at various rates of inflation. Here's another look at how that works: If the rate of inflation were to average 3 percent during your lifetime, the cost of living would double every 24 years (72 ÷ 3 = 24). That means if you are 35 years old today, have an after-tax income of $40,000 that you spend every red cent of, when you're 59 years old, you'll need an after-tax income of $80,000 just to keep up with your current standard of living!

If inflation were to jump up and average 6 percent, your cost of living would double every 12 years. Yikes!

So with prices on most of the goods and services we buy more often than not on the rise, saving and investing for our futures needs to become as essential in every one of our lives as learning to walk.

Investing for Your Life Stage: The Twenties

Profile: Marie and Ralph Johnson

Marie and Ralph are in their late twenties. They're both working, have been married for a year and a half, have no children, and live in a rented two-bedroom condominium. Together their annual salaries amount to roughly $50,000.

While their near-term personal goals include buying a home and then having a family, saving money is a "talked about" priority for this couple. So instead of finding its way into savings bonds or savings accounts, their disposable income gets spent on things like Super Nintendo, big-screen TVs, tickets to sporting events, eating out, and vacationing.

What's typical about couples like Marie and Ralph is they are spending all of their disposable income even though Marie admits that they could easily save $200 a month—"even $500 if we put our mind to it."

The good news for this couple, and many other double-income twenty-something pairs, is that with a minimal amount of effort these two young people can create a very handsome retirement nest egg for themselves.

Keeping in mind that being a good money manager means saving for near- and short-term goals *and* saving for retirement, here's how this couple can begin creating a nice retirement nest egg for themselves.

Their first step is easy. Since both are working, each needs to find out what kind, if any, of qualified retirement plans is available to them and then participate in it. Ralph, for instance, works for a large grocery store chain that offers its employees a 401(k). Currently he's not participating in that qualified retirement plan and he should be. Marie's company doesn't offer a retirement plan, which means she's got to create one on her own. Starting an IRA is a good place for her to begin.

FICA taxes are taken out of both Ralph and Marie's checks. That means each is earning quarters of credit which can make them eligible for Social Security insurance later in life.

The next step is to look at some savings goals—both short- and long-term. For example, if Marie and Ralph were to save only $200 a month, invest half of it, $100, into a well-heeled growth mutual fund ear-marked for retirement, and keep investing that same amount of money faithfully each month for the next 35 years, reinvesting all capital gains and income and being taxed at a 28 percent level annually on the growth of the fund, they would have invested a total of $42,000 and have a nest egg of

- $230,918, provided their investment had an average annual total return of 8 percent.

- $382,828 if their investment had an average annual total return of 10 percent.

- $649,527 if their money worked for them at an average annual rate of 12 percent.

That's a pretty nifty-sized nest egg at any level!

The second half of that $200—or $100 a month—needs to be saved for immediate and short-term needs. Saving $100 a month in a savings account or interest-bearing checking account until it grows to $500 or $1000 is a good goal to have. At those higher levels, people can open money-market mutual funds, which pay higher interest rates than simple savings accounts do. Or they might want to invest in CDs or Treasury bonds.

Or if Ralph and Marie would save approximately 10 percent of their incomes, say, $500 a month, and place $400 into a short-term savings account and $100 into a long-term investment like a mutual fund earmarked for their retirement, at the end of twelve months their savings would total $4800 plus what was earned in interest.

At that rate, in two years this couple could have enough money for a downpayment on their first home. Or, they would have a personal savings account that's substantial. Or they would have enough money to start building a substantial investment portfolio of their own: 100 shares of a $15-a-share stock is only $1500.

No matter how you slice it, all Marie and Ralph have to do is to start saving money *today* and stay in that habit, then their concerns about where the money to fund their short-term wants and long-term goals won't be a worry.

Must-Have Checklist for This Decade

An absolute must at this stage is a savings account. If possible at an FDIC-insured bank.

Get into the habit early of rewarding yourself for the work you do. That means, ideally taking 10 percent right off the top of your paycheck each and every time you receive one. It doesn't really matter if that 10 percent comes off the gross pay received or the net amount. What matters is that you get into the habit of paying yourself. If 10 percent is too much to handle, try 5 percent.

Savings account yields are always going to be low, but you absolutely, positively need some kind of savings vehicle, if you are actively going to begin investing for your retirement. There are no ifs, ands, or buts about it.

Savings accounts—even if they start out as cookie jars—are accumulation spots. They help us get into the habit of saving money and show us how quickly money can grow if we only add to it. They also are the easiest way in which to build up ready-cash reserves to use to pay for those unexpected bills that come our way—like the new set of tires you need for your car—or for the things you want—like a new home, or the zillion and one different things that you'd like to have.

Be careful, though. Sometimes savings accounts can be expensive to maintain, as banks often charge fees for accounts that don't have much money in them. If that's the story at your bank, start saving money in your own private bank: the "cookie jar" bank at home.

Once you've accumulated, say, $500 or $1000 and would like a little more return from your savings account monies, check into money-market funds. These are available either at your bank or via a mutual fund family. The ones from your bank are called money-market deposit accounts, and the monies invested in them may be insured, if the bank is an FDIC-insured bank; ones from mutual funds are called money-market mutual funds, and they are *not* insured. Both provide relatively quick access to your money and have no sales charge fees associated with them.

What Makes Good Sense

- Limit the number of credit cards you have to less than a handful and then pay off all other credit card debt. No one needs to be paying interest charges of 16, 18, or 22 percent on credit card debt.

- Ask your employer about the retirement benefits packages he or she makes available. Once you've found out what, if any, retirement plans are in place—like a 401(k) or a stock option plan, take the time to learn about each program and then begin participating as soon as possible.

- Check into opening an IRA for yourself even if the money that you contribute to it isn't deductible from your taxes. Money can grow like wildflowers when given a chance to compound tax-deferred on its own. (A word of caution: Again, make sure to check into any fees involved with opening and maintaining an IRA account. If the fees are high, and the amount invested small, IRA investing might not make sense.)

  If you're self-employed, open a SEP-IRA or Keogh. Contributions here can make a difference in your annual tax consequences today and your retirement lifestyle tomorrow.

- Look at your insurance options. See if homeowner or renter's insurance and disability insurance are things you need. Make sure to review both your automobile and medical insurance coverage (if you plan on having kids, check to see if pregnancies and childbirth costs are covered) and see what kinds of life policies may be appropriate for your needs. Remember not to let insurance costs get out of hand. Not everyone needs all types of insurance coverage.

Where and How to Invest Monies

When the time horizon for investing is a long one, as it would be if you were to start investing for your retirement in your twenties, most financial experts suggest investing aggressively. This, as you might guess, is going to mean something different to everyone.

So, because what looks aggressive to one person may look conservative to another, what's important to learn right now is what the various investment products are and how each works. This information will give you a sense of how investment products differ, and it will also help you to choose which investments to put your money into.

To begin this learning process, eyeball the investment arena and come up with some products that appeal to you. Then ask your broker, insurance agent, or financial planner for more information on each, making sure to look at their risk and reward potentials. The smarter you are about an investment product, the easier creating an investment portfolio for your retirement will be.

The Beauty and the Beastly (Sides to Retirement Investing in Your Twenties)

The beauty of saving, then investing, for your retirement when you're in your twenties is *time.*

Thanks to compounding, a relatively modest IRA investment made in, and only in, your twenties could grow, by your sixties, to substantially more monies than you would have received had you started investing later and contributed every year until retirement. (See the inset in Chapter 3, "Start Now," to see how this is done.) The sooner you start socking money away for the long-term, the better your results are likely to be.

The beast in saving early is that it seems like no fun.

There's something about saving money that can feel like a drag—especially when you're young and there seem to be so many other fun ways to spend money, like on clothes, cosmetics, shoes, vacations, or gym equipment, not to mention a new car or boat.

But there is also nothing like the "feel" of money in the bank, as opposed to the "feeling" of living from paycheck to paycheck. I know both feelings well. And I prefer—as well as recommend—the first.

So, to save yourself some stress, and to help create some wealth, get into the habit of chipping off 10 percent of the money you receive from your employer and putting it into a savings account. Do this if for no other reason than to make yourself feel good.

A BRIGHT IDEA

Here's a two-fisted savings account idea. Consider your right hand to be the one that's in control of your money needs now and your left hand in control of the money earmarked for long-term investing.

In the right-handed account, or the near- to short-term account, start saving money for a rainy day—or for those unexpected expensive days that might come along. This will be the your cash reserves account that—once it grows—will form the base for all your other short- and medium-term wants and needs.

To make this account grow, add to it often. Left unattended, short-term savings plans can lose their appeal. But when added to on a regular basis, they can change your life.

In the left-handed account, the long-term and retirement one, consider taking some risks; try investing aggressively with a portion of this money. Because this account may have 20, 30, or 40 years in which to grow, make sure some portion of the money gets placed into investments with a solid history of growth.

Investing for Your Life Stage: The Thirties

Profile: Catherine and Ronald Baker

Ron is 38-year-old physician. His wife, Catherine, a homemaker. They've got two daughters, ages 3 and 10; live in a new home with a fat mortgage; and he's got student loan payments—along with car payments—to make each month.

The retirement investing that Ron has done so far is focused around his medical practice; he's a partner in a medical group. He's also invested in a universal life insurance policy that he hopes will pay for his daughters' college educations, and has term life insurance to cover immediate needs if he should die suddenly. And that's it.

Dee Lee is a certified financial planner and registered investment advisor in Harvard, Massachusetts. She thinks that Ron might be wise to look again at that universal life policy he's hoping will cover the costs of his daughters' future educations.

"The insurance company is investing the money for you and charging a very large fee to do so," Lee says. "Plus the projected growth numbers from policies generally aren't guaranteed. . . ."

Because of those two factors, Lee recommends that Ron review his commitment to the universal life policy, check out the rate at which his money is growing, and if it's not to his liking, perhaps decrease the amount he's paying into it, keeping the minimal insurance portions of this policy along with keeping the term life policy. She thinks the money saved from this change ought to go into stock fund investments.

"Life insurance should be used to cover the loss of an income stream or to leave as an inheritance," says Lee. "But not as an investment vehicle."

Ron also said that he'd like to start saving $300 a month for his retirement. This figure represents less than 3 percent of his gross income.

"If they look at their budget closely, there are probably many ways that they can save on expenses and increase their savings," adds Lee.

She suggests that Ron and Catherine keep a detailed budget for several months to see how and where they spend their money. "How they are spending their money is very important. Oftentimes, the more we make, the less discipline we have."

Since the mortgage on the Bakers' home is an adjustable one, and they plan on living in that home for many years to come, Lee thinks they ought to consider refinancing and going with a fixed rate.

Disability insurance is also something that the Bakers ought to consider, as is taking full advantage of individual and spousal IRAs. And Ron's group practice ought to consider a 401(k) retirement plan or profit-sharing plan if at all feasible.

Must-Have Checklist for This Decade

- A savings account. If it's at a bank, check to see if it's insured.

- And/or a money-market account

What Makes Good Sense

- Open an IRA.

- Don't get into credit card debt. Even though we now are able to pay our taxes with credit cards—then earn frequent-flyer miles from the airlines for doing so—that's probably not the wisest financial planning move (unless you can afford to pay off the tax debt in one month). In other words, don't get hooked into making small payments at big interest rates. Credit card debt can ruin anyone's financial health. Be wary of it.

- Participate in your company's pension benefits program. If you don't know, or understand, what retirement benefits your firm offers, ask your boss or contact the individual within your company in charge of employee benefits. Or get in touch with your company's human resources department. If you're self-employed, check out the benefits of tax-deferred planning vehicles like SEP-IRAs or Keoghs.

- Depending upon your family situation, and whether you are married or not or have children, consult your insurance representative and ask about the different policies—including disability insurance—he or she has available that might be appropriate for your current needs.

- Now is also the time, if you haven't done so already, to begin investing money independently of the "qualified" kinds of retirement vehicles available to you. To gain as much financial independence as possible, create your own individual portfolio of perhaps individual stocks or bonds, and mutual funds or insurance products. A well-constructed personal portfolio means you won't have to depend totally on your firm's retirement benefits program and Social Security for your income during retirement. Without those financial worries, it will be easier to spend your days fishing, gardening, volunteering, playing with your grandchildren, or just doing nothing at all.

Where and How to Invest Monies

Again, the pat answer heard from professionals as to where and how to invest is still "more aggressively than conservatively."

If, for example, you're 37 years old and are just beginning to save for your retirement, there is still plenty of time for that money to grow—provided it's given a chance.

Monies can remain invested in qualified retirement plans until you reach age 70½. So, if you're 37 today and plan on letting your retirement money work for you as long as possible, that money has about 33 years in which to grow and compound tax-deferred.

The Beauty and the Beastly (Sides to Retirement Investing in Your Thirties)

Time here is again the beauty.

Given that the performance of the stock market runs in cycles—each varying in length typically from about three to seven years—taking advantage of the growth opportunities within the stock market, particularly when your investment horizon is out over 30 years, is definitely worth considering. Therefore, don't rule out the stock market when time is on your side.

The beastly side of investing in your thirties is life's expenses. So many things happen to people in their thirties that didn't necessarily happen to them in their twenties.

Lots of people who aren't already married, get married. Many have kids or buy homes, cars, boats, take vacations, send kids to the dentist or summer camp, pay for preschools and private schools. All of which involve, more often than not, out-of-pocket expenses that weren't necessarily anticipated.

But no matter what your life's circumstances are—whether you're caught in a money crunch needing more accessible cash or not—do the best you can to continue to pay yourself first.

And don't stop taking advantage of the retirement plans offered to you via your employer—or the ones you created if you're self-employed.

Saving money can be downright difficult, if not seem impossible, to do at times. When it seems impossible to do, try as best you can to remain on the investment track that you've begun. If you fall off that path, get back up and start again.

Investing for Your Life Stage: The Forties

Profile: Barbara Meredith

Barbara Meredith was 46 years old when her husband Bob died. He died suddenly, leaving Barbara not only in shock but unprepared financially for her future.

Bob did not have any life insurance policies to provide Barbara with any kind of income after his death. Nor had he accumulated enough quarters of credit from Social Security for her to be able to receive monthly income checks from that federal agency. And, like many couples whose spouses are self-employed entrepreneurs, the cash-flow problems of small business ownerships often mean cash-flow problems at home. This was the case in the Meredith household.

But there's always a bright side to every set of circumstances. In this case it was Barbara's courage—and her nursing career—that in time turned a debt-filled situation into an asset-growing one.

After Bob's death, Barbara was swamped with debts: funeral expenses, business debts, and her own debts. To get out from under this sea of "pay-me's," a few months after her husband's death, Barbara enrolled in a six-weekend financial planning course offered at a local community college. It was via that course that she learned all about personal money management, the importance of various kinds of insurance policies, and the difference between investment products.

After the course ended, Barbara put into practice many of the things she'd learned.

"I started with a minimum fifty-dollar-a-month contribution into the Janus Fund seven years ago," she says, "Some months I'd throw in more if I could. And I can't believe how much that account has grown in value too."

The Janus Fund is just one of the mutual funds Barbara has invested into and only one of the investments that she has made after her husband's death. She also has done things like purchased a disability insurance plan, started a payroll deduction plan, and opened an IRA. And she says, "I worked my tail off." Today, thanks to all of her efforts, she has a personal portfolio valued at over $70,000, created in just seven years.

How'd she do that? The key to Barbara's investment success has three parts to it:

1. It began with her personal conviction to get out of the jam she was in.
2. Then she acted on that conviction and enrolled in a financial planning course.
3. And it has ended with her discipline to create a personal financial plan and then follow through with it.

"I've had to make a lot of changes in the way I spend money and how I think about money," says this now 53-year-old. "But it has been worth every bit of it. Not only do I have money in the bank. I've got a portfolio of stocks that are making me money!"

Must-Have Checklist for This Decade

- A savings account, set up through an FDIC-insured bank, credit union, or both
- One or more money-market accounts
- An investment portfolio of your own, one that is independent of any qualified retirement plans. This portfolio can be made up of virtually anything of value. If you owr investments like stocks, bonds, or mutual funds, they naturally would be a part of your personal portfolio. So would the collectibles you've acquired that have value or that 1964 Mustang you keep under wraps in the garage.
- Part-time cottage industries and sideline businesses can also be a part of your own personal portfolio.

What Makes Good Sense

- Get out of debt: credit card, student loans, personal debt. Whatever it is, make sure you're working your way out of it now.
- Contribute as much as possible to your company defined contribution plans—like a 401(k) and 403(b) plans—if they offer one.
- Have monies taken out via a payroll deduction plan if one is available to you and earmark those dollars for retirement.
- Keep contributing to your IRAs, SEP-IRAs, and Keoghs.
- Look at and review any insurance policies that you may have. Then ask yourself if they are necessary and are meeting your needs, or if there are changes that ought to be made in them.

Where and How to Invest Monies

By the time you've reached age 40, you've been an adult for about one-half of your life. And if you're one of the fortunate who has been saving money and investing it over the past two decades, you've probably accumulated a pretty nifty-sized nest egg. Looking at the savings/investment path that you've taken and reviewing your investment decisions now makes good sense.

If trying to build a nest egg hasn't been possible for you so far, this is the decade to kick in and create a retirement savings plan as soon as possible. But make sure the plan you create is something that's workable.

Here's a look at how three different monthly money amounts can grow and compound tax-deferred in the years ahead. If you're 45 and put $100 a month away into a tax-deferred account that earns an average of 8 percent for the next 20 years, the value of that investment will be just over $59,000 when you reach age 65. By upping that monthly contribution to $300, in 20 years of tax-deferred growth and compounding it will amount to about $178,000. A monthly investment of $500 a month would bring it to $296,000. (The previous figures are all from the Scudder Retirement Plans calculator.)

Usually it's in their forties when people realize a couple of things: first, life is short. And second, retirement isn't all that far away.

What you do about the first realization could change how you live your day-to-day life. As far as the second one goes, if your plan is to build a six-figure-size nest egg, it's going to take more than a few dollars invested here and there. It's going to take real commitment and discipline.

The Beauty and the Beastly (Sides to Retirement Investing in Your Forties)

Time is still on your side—but only about half as much as it was 20 years ago. That means that you've got to focus on your retirement savings goals. On the other hand, if you have 10, 15, or 20 years of retirement savings and investing experience under your belt—you're probably in Happy Land, amazed at how easy it was to amass major money and wondering why everybody doesn't have a huge retirement savings.

The beastly side of the forties can be like those of the previous decade—divorces, life changes, and big-time expenses. If you got married and had children when you were in your twenties, there can be the costs of your kid's weddings to contend with, along with their school and college expenses. Then there is the high cost of a divorce, emotionally as well as financially.

People in their forties often have parents, grandparents, other adults or grown children who they also must care for. So the costs for more mouths to feed can be high.

If you've been a planner and strategizer, these expenses might not be a drain on your savings or investment gains. Then again, they could put you into debt—more debt than you'd hoped to have at this point in your life.

Should you find yourself in a debt-filled position in your forties, go back to square one and begin paying yourself first. Then, work at paying off those debts. There's a rhythm to saving money, investing, and distributing your wealth. It begins with paying yourself first.

Investing for Your Life Stage: The Fifties

Profile: Marjorie and Jack Kroger

It was a surprise to the Krogers when the electric utility company that Jack worked for offered him an early retirement package.

"Retiring early is something I never really thought much about," says this 52-year-old father of three.

But when he and his wife looked at the early retirement package offered, they saw it both as an opportunity to have a bundle of money to invest and as a chance for each to do something new and different with their lives.

Prior to taking early retirement, Jack and Marjorie had done little to save for retirement. Both had worked, so they knew that Social Security would be a source of income in their old age. But the high cost of putting three kids through college, weddings, and now taking care of Jack's father meant that all their disposable income got spent.

One preretirement move that Jack and Marjorie made was to sell the home their kids grew up in and take the proceeds from that sale to buy the home that they hope to live the rest of their lives in. Although the money from the sale of their first home didn't foot the entire bill for the cost of the second, it provided them with a large downpayment and hence a mortgage they expect to have paid off in about a dozen years.

"A mortgage-free home is a retiree's trump card," says Jonathan Pond, a financial adviser in Watertown, Massachusetts. "Absent the mortgage means your retirement income requirements are 15, 20, or maybe even 25 percent lower than they would be were you burdened with a mortgage or rent."

Right now Jack's retired officially but working part-time as a consultant. He realized that the early retirement package offered him provided an ample amount of cash and medical coverage but that the money received wasn't enough to last his entire life. So, he took a lion's share of the money and invested that into mutual funds. His time horizon for needing the money from those funds is in 10 years. That's when he hopes to fully retire.

According to Terry Savage, a financial columnist and investment advisor, that time horizon is a very optimistic one. "Ten years is far too short a time horizon."

She explained that just as the Dow Jones Industrial Average rose from under 1000 in 1982 to 3700 in 1993, it can also fall. "People have found out that home prices don't always go up. They are also going to find that stock prices don't always go up."

Retirement planning suggestions for the Krogers include building up their liquid cash reserves and making sure that this short-term pot is large enough to cover one to two years' worth of mortgage and car payments. And it also includes stretching out the length of time they've targeted their mutual fund investments to work within. Moving it from a 10- to a 15-year time horizon would be wise.

Must-Have Checklist for This Decade

- An insured savings account, or two or three
- Money-market account(s)
- An investment portfolio of your own independent of the qualified retirement plans that your employer—or the one your own company—has provided you with

- An estate plan that—at the very least—includes a will

What Makes Sense

- If your company's retirement plans include defined contribution plans—like 401(k)s or 403(b)s—which you can contribute to, continue to add as much money as possible to these programs. Don't forget to review the investments selected in your employer-sponsored retirement plans periodically.

  Keep adding, whenever possible, to your IRA, SEP-IRA, or Keogh accounts.

- Disability insurance is expensive at this age. But it may be necessary. If you find out you don't need this coverage any longer, redirect the monies you have been spending on that monthly policy into a long-term investing plan.

- Start to do some concrete estate planning. If you haven't already, create a will, or set up trust accounts, for you and your spouse. Or at least begin thinking about your estate and how you wish to have it handled.

- Contact Social Security for an idea of the amount of payments you're likely to receive from that agency when you decide to retire. And use this information to help gauge what tack to take when allocating and investing your monies.

- Set up a long-term health-care fund. Start looking at supplementing health-care coverage plans to cover both the gaps in Medicare and the cost of long-term nursing-home care.

- This is the age some investors consider purchasing tax-deferred investments such as tax-free bonds; redirect the assets in their personal portfolios; contribute as much as possible to their 401(k) monies; and if they haven't established one already, begin building an investment portfolio.

Trying to estimate how much money you'll have—along with how much money you'll need to have—by the time you retire are questions that become easier to answer when you're in your fifties, especially for those choosing to retire early, say at age 59½ or 60.

If you're planning an early retirement, meet with your company's benefits coordinator to get an idea of how much money their retirement program will provide. And talk with your accountant, stockbroker, or financial planner to help calculate what your tax bracket might be at retirement and the kinds of income your investments might provide.

Retiring around the age of 60 means understanding that whatever monies are available to you are probably going to have to last for the next 20 if not 30 years or more.

For those not planning on retiring at the end of this decade, you've got until age 70½ in which to salt money away in qualified retirement plans. When considering any new investment, investigate the expenses and commission costs. Those fees can be costly and eat into the performance of your investment choices.

Where and How to Invest Monies

In a word, "carefully."

Even though your lifeline gets longer the longer you live, chances are you won't work throughout all of the years that lie ahead. That makes the fifties a great time for review. At this point, retirement isn't just a far-off notion, it's a real issue. During this decade take the time to sit down to review the assets you have accumulated and to see if your investing style (a) has been rewarding, and (b) is still appropriate. If not, change it. Alter the asset mix if you must, keeping in mind that some small investment percentage changes can mean a big difference in financial rewards.

The Beauty and the Beastly (Sides to Retirement Investing in Your Fifties)

Most of the beauty of retirement saving in the fifties is for people who started saving and investing early or who were fortunate enough to have made some wise business decisions during the previous decades. If you are one of those individuals, you probably have a whopper-sized net worth by now.

But if you're like most people, who, according to recent reports have about $5000 in the bank and the only retirement savings plan they are involved with is the one they have at work, it's in the fifties that you'll hear a loud retirement planning "WAKE UP" call.

Time and money can be fickle friends in this decade. Money, given lots of time to compound, can grow into large amounts even when it's invested conservatively. Money given less time to compound isn't as likely to grow as much unless it's invested more aggressively. If your goal is to accumulate "lots of money" and you're just beginning a retirement investing plan now, reaching that goal will probably mean taking more risks with the investment money available to you.

So, depending upon what you've done in the past, the fifties are generally the time when the piper begins to get paid.

For some, that might mean investing more conservatively; for others staying on course with their plans; and for still others going gang-busters and trying to grab all the financial gusto that they can.

If you're in that last category, try not to let your enthusiasm for making money overshadow the risks involved. And don't lose hope. There still is time to make money and sound investments.

Investing for Your Life Stage: The Sixties

Profile: Eileen Marshall

Eileen Marshall retired four years ago when she was 62. She'd been a schoolteacher for 20 years, not joining the work force until her three children were all in school.

Like Barbara, Eileen was also a widow in her forties. Unlike Barbara, Eileen didn't ever care much for learning about investing or investments. So her part in her own retirement planning has been minimal.

"I just don't have an interest in financial things. I'd rather be home spending time with my grandchildren than worrying about money."

Currently, Eileen's income comes from Social Security and her teacher's pension. Together that provides her with about the same amount of monthly income that her teaching job did.

Other assets that she has include her home, which is paid for, two annuities, some CDs, and a savings account. Eileen guestimates her net worth, excluding the value of her home, to be around $75,000.

Most financial planners hearing Eileen's story shudder. They think she'll outlive her nest egg. And they also fear that, because she doesn't want to invest in growth kinds of securities, she'll either have to alter her lifestyle in the future or go back into the work force. Both of which may or may not be true.

Eileen's lifestyle is simple yet comfortable. She knows how she likes to live and what she likes to do with her time. She also knows how to budget her money and, as they say, stretch a buck. Her lifestyle along with life choices stand as reminders that there is no one-sized nest egg sum that fits all of us.

While the biggest money concerns that Eileen has are health-related—fearing that one day she might not be able to take care of herself or cover the rapidly rising costs of medical care and coverage—she lives one day at a time and is enjoying every bit of her life.

So, while this retiree isn't really concerned about inflation, or the potential loss of buying power in her retirement portfolio, she is also not worried about tomorrow. "Everything has a way of working out."

We'll have to check back with Eileen in 5, 10, or 20 years to see how she's doing.

Must-Have Checklist for This Decade

- An insured savings account(s)
- A money-market account or two
- An investment portfolio made up of securities independent of your company pension plan
- Your estate plans in order

What Makes Good Sense

- Keep adding to those tax-deferred opportunities that come your way, from your company's 401(k) or 403(b) plans to annuities. At the max, there are still $10\frac{1}{2}$ years—until age $70\frac{1}{2}$—to contribute to an IRA, SEP-IRA, or Keogh.
- Contact Social Security and Medicare to find out about the benefits each can provide, if you haven't retired yet.
- Make sure to investigate gap insurance for Medicare and long-term nursing-care coverage.
- Talk to your financial planner, estate planner, or accountant about the lifestyle changes you may be thinking about. Look to them for answers about the financial bottom lines of retirement—for instance, deciding the age at which to retire; what to do with lump-sum payouts; or how to gift money to your children or favorite charity.

Where and How to Invest Monies

Carefully.

Sixty-year-olds easily have another two or three decades of investing time ahead of them. They also may have personal health problems, careers that have been cut short, and children and in-laws that may need their financial assistance. How aggressively they invest will depend upon the variables in their lives and their own individual investment tastes.

"I've got a client who's eighty years old and only invests in stocks," says Mark Scheinbaum, manager of Furhman-Matt Securities in Boca Raton, Florida.

While investing all of your money totally in stocks is not the norm for most sixty- or eightysomethings, financial experts do suggest that a portion of one's investing cash be in the stock market in this sixth decade of your life.

Asset shifting in this decade might mean moving some monies out of taxable securities and investing them into tax-free bonds. Along with moving a portion of one's mutual fund stock portfolios from growth into growth and income kinds of funds.

The bottom line on sixties investing is that this is a time to look out toward that upcoming life change: Retirement. It doesn't matter if you're going to retire at 62, 65, 75, or 90. What matters is realizing that whatever money is within reach for you today will more than likely make up the foundation of the money that will have to last you . . . a lifetime.

The Beauty and the Beastly (Sides to Retirement Investing in Your Sixties)

The beauty part to this stage in life is that by now you probably know yourself pretty well. You know your spending style, your lifestyle habits, the clothes you like to wear, and the cars you prefer to drive. Plus, you know how to manage money, whether you realize it or not. After all, you've been doing so for decades.

What comes with all this experience and wisdom is knowing how much money you can live on. A comfortable retirement nest egg to some people in their sixties today might be anywhere from $20,000 to $40,000. For others it needs to be hundreds of thousands or even millions of dollars.

The beastly side of the sixties is again the time factor. During your twenties, thirties, and forties, investing time was on your side. When you're in your fifties, sixties, seventies, eighties, and nineties, even though the time is there, your willingness to take risks might not be. That's not to say that fortunes can't be made. Hardly. Some have made millions during their golden years.

So if your goal is to be a multi-million-dollar entrepreneur and you still believe that you've got a reasonable shot at attaining that goal, go for it! Accomplishments happen at all different ages. But investments and investment products still perform in their own cycles.

That means, if you're 67 today and figure on living another 25 years, whatever percentage of total assets that you have invested in stocks could probably go through no less than three market cycles during that time period.

On the other hand, if you've never been a fan of the stock market, choosing to invest only in long-term bonds for the income they provide could cost some buying power problems 20 or 30 years from now.

The real beast of the sixties, and even the seventies and eighties, is realizing that answering tough financial questions like, "Where do I invest and how much should I put into stocks or bonds?" never gets any easier the older you get. Hopefully what does get easier with age is understanding and accepting that everything changes—including money, markets, and one's financial needs.

Investing for Your Life Stage: The Seventies

Profile: Connie and William McCormick

Connie and William are newlyweds. They've only been married for three years, both are now 75 years old, and it's a second marriage for each.

Second marriages bring to the retirement planning table a host of new circumstances. For these two people, drawing up a prenuptial agreement was something both opted for.

"We each have grown children who we want to pass our investments on to when we die," says Connie. "And the smartest way for us to do that was to create our own prenuptial this-is-mine kind of agreement."

What's interesting about this couple is how differently each prepared for their retirements. In Connie's first marriage she was a homemaker. It wasn't until she was in her forties that she joined the work force as a secretary. Investing for her and her first husband meant "saving" only.

After her husband's death, and with the guidance of her employer, Connie started working with a stockbroker and learned about how important diversification was. Today, her own personal retirement portfolio includes dividend-producing blue-chip stocks, mutual funds, and zero-coupon bonds.

William, on the other hand, doesn't have a diversified securities portfolio. He never felt as though he understood the stock market, so any investments that he and his first wife made were either in bank CDs or in real estate. Together they bought and renovated homes, typically converting them into income-producing properties.

William's retirement plans included holding on to these properties and then using the income from them as his source of retirement income. Although his plan is working, rising property taxes and maintenance costs are eating into his monthly income.

Together this couple lives comfortably on their combined Social Security and pension incomes. Each saves and invests for the future independently.

They both agree that they spend more money in retirement than they did when each was working. "You've got much more time on your hands and there's so much to do, of course we spend more," comments Connie.

Rising health-care costs are a primary concern for the McCormicks—as is the rising cost of living. According to William, "Things don't get cheaper when you retire, they get more expensive."

Must-Have Checklist for This Decade

- A savings account—or two, or three, or four. Each should be in banks or institutions offering FDIC insurance and with account balances of less than $100,000 so that each can be in fully insured accounts.

- A money-market account or two, including a tax-free money-market account, if your tax bracket warrants it.

- An investment portfolio that's tuned into your income needs. Most likely that will be one that provides a steady stream of income, still grows in value, and is easy on your tax bill.

- Your estate planning ought to be in order with wills and personal plans regarding your health and funeral decisions talked about as well as written out.

What Makes Good Sense

- Balance your books. Since this is typically the draw-down stage of life—when the pensions, Social Security, and the retirement plans you've created start to provide you with an income—getting the most out of your money now means keeping good track of where it comes from—and where it goes to.

- Keep working with a financial planner, investment advisor, or your accountant. Tax laws, and markets, change every year. Many of those changes can affect your annual spendable income. So keeping in touch with the financial experts could keep your retirement nest egg in the black.

- Consider taking advantage of the tax benefits allowed when gifting money to your family, friends, or charity.

- Put your personal house in order. Have you made a will yet? If not, do so. Or check to see if the one created still meets your wishes. Is a living will something you would like to have? Make sure to have one good Medicare-gap policy, and long-term nursing-care coverage. Think about your lifestyle needs. Are they changing? Do you want to live in another part of the country or world? Would you like to move into an adult-care, health-care, or retirement property?

Where and How to Invest Monies

I'd like to say, "Anyway you want!" But unless you've accumulated millions, your lifeline could be longer than you ever imagined. Consequently, you'll probably still have to invest for tomorrow. How to do that will depend upon things like the size of your personal and financial estate; your tax bracket; what you want to do with the 10, 20, or even 30 years ahead of you; your health; and whether or not you want to spend all the money that's come your way before you die or distribute it.

Investing in your seventies, then, means having an investment time horizon that's uncertain. It could be one that looks out a few years or a couple of decades. Whatever your vantage point is, don't overlook the cost of living—just like our age, it typically only gets higher and higher.

Watch out not to box yourself into an income stream that's permanently fixed—and doesn't allow for some growth of principal.

The Beauty and the Beastly
(Sides to Retirement Investing in
Your Seventies)

The beauty of this decade is that no matter how much money you've been able to squirrel away, the experiences that you've had during your 70 years are worth 10 million times more. Share—if not sell—those tales whenever possible.

The beastly side is the real possibility of outliving your money. With your death date sometime out in the future and your income stream more than likely tuned into your current needs, managing money for the future takes discipline—the same discipline it took to save the money.

18
In the End

Behold the turtle: He only makes progress
when he sticks his neck out.

JAMES BRYANT CONANT

Investing for your retirement means sticking your neck out and taking financial responsibility today for something that's going to happen to you in the distant future.

Not knowing the exact date of our retirements, whether or not we'll have enough money to retire on, whether or not we will live long enough to retire, or how the investments that we've made will pay off are, quite often, reasons enough to keep our heads in the sand regarding retirement issues—or, in the case of the turtle, our necks tucked safely inside our shells.

But avoiding the money side of retirement is one sure way to almost guarantee that those golden years could be financially difficult ones.

If you have ever lived through the emotional stress of not knowing where the money is going to come from to buy groceries, provide your child with lunch money, pay the rent, or put gas in your car, you have a sense of how difficult life can be for the financially strapped in their retirement.

"Retirement is great," says a retiree from Cleveland. "I just wish I had the money to enjoy it."

As you've learned throughout the chapters of this book, having money to spend during retirement involves taking advantage of the retirement benefits plans your employer offers, if your employer offers them; creating plans for yourself if you're self-employed and making sure to pay the FICA tax; and then saving and investing on your own. Money to spend during retirement can also come to you if you marry well, inherit a bundle, win the lottery, or keep on working.

If you choose not to retire, the seventies, eighties, and nineties could be the richest times of your life. Someone who is 75 and still working full-time is not only collecting a paycheck, but he or she is also collecting Social Security along with the monies from any investments made in things like an IRA, SEP-IRA, Keogh, and even some annuities. So for the geriatric worker, life could be financially very rewarding.

But if the thought of working later in life isn't in your long-term plans, be a trend-setter; start aggressively saving for your retirement as soon as you turn 21 or accept your first job. Chances are you'll be glad you did.

Coming Up Short

What happens if you're nearing retirement age and the nest egg you'd hoped to create isn't quite fat enough to carry you? Here are five suggestions to help you deal with that situation.

1. *Retire later.* There's no law saying that retirement must begin by such-and-such an age. If you haven't accumulated enough money to retire, work longer.

2. *Save more today.* If it looks as though you won't have the money you'd hoped for, start saving more right now. Sacrificing a little in your lifestyle today could make retiring tomorrow a lot easier.

3. *Reduce your goal.* Take a second look at the financial nest egg goal that you've set for yourself. Maybe you don't need as big a nest egg as you'd thought.

4. *Take some risks.* Reevaluate the kinds of investments that you've made with your retirement monies. If they are all conservative ones, perhaps a little bit more risk with a small percentage of your total holdings might just be the ticket that will bolster the overall performance of all your investments.

5. *Work part-time.* Lots of retirees supplement their income—and enhance their lifestyles—by working part-time. It's an option to always keep open for yourself.

The Last Words

Throughout this book the goal has been to make sure that you start the retirement planning, saving, and investing process on the right foot. Now in conclusion, here are some final tips for staying on the right track to building a successful retirement investment plan.

- Make "smart money" decisions. We've all heard Wall Street pundits talk about where the smart money gets invested. When it comes to you and your retirement, the smartest money move of all is to take control of your financial future by making sure that each and every month some monies get added to your retirement kitty.

  Even when times are tough and the monthly bills are higher than your monthly income, see to it that at least $1 goes into your retirement fund. After all, initially it's not the size of the contribution as much as it is getting into the habit of saving for your future that counts the most.

- Look for opportunities. Believe it or not, you do have quite a bit of control when it comes to securing a solid financial future for your retirement years. Along with saving and investing on your own, take full advantage of what your employer offers. If they have a 401(k) plan in place, contribute the maximum. If your employer matches contributions, all the better. The bottom line is adjust your spending and saving patterns so that you do build a retirement nest egg.

- Think *big* and think long term. Many people fall into the trap of making short-term investment decisions when they still have 10, 20, 30, or more years in which to invest. Consequently, they may put their money exclusively into short-term certificates of deposit (CDs) or money-market accounts, neither of which provide the growth potential necessary to outpace inflation and help ensure that they won't outlive their nest egg.

- Accept the challenge of inflation and combat it. Over the last 20 years inflation has averaged 5.9 percent. At that rate what costs $10 today will cost $20 in 12 years. Any inflation rate, even those averaging 3 or 4 percent annually, can whittle away the contents of a nest egg. For instance, over 10 years, a 4 percent annual inflation rate can reduce the value of $100,000 to $66,483. At 6 percent inflation over 15 years that $100,000 is worth only $39,529. Look for investment products that have historically beaten inflation rates, then select some— ones you're comfortable with and understand—to invest in.

- Consider taking some calculated risks. As emphasized throughout this book, no investments are totally risk-free. Even with savings accounts, there is the risk that the interest earned from those accounts will not keep pace with inflation. Once you've accepted the reality that all investing involves some risk, investigate thoroughly the risk factors associated with different investments.

Taking calculated investment risks isn't the same as throwing caution to the wind—or taking a risk just for the thrill of it. Taking calculated investment risks begins with doing your homework, and ends with making educated choices. Try it.

- Plan on your plans changing. Everything changes, sometimes quickly, sometimes slowly. At whatever speed, change happens. And there is no denying that changing interest rates, changing stock and bond prices, and changes in our life circumstances can sometimes throw a monkey wrench into the best-laid long-term retirement plans. But change also breeds opportunity. Take advantage of the changes in your life and look for the opportunity each brings.

Epilogue

When I began writing this book, there was very little simple, common-sense literature available for those wanting to start a retirement investment program for themselves. Today that's not the case.

As the millions of baby boomers near retirement age, more and more financial institutions—such as banks, brokerage firms, insurance companies, and mutual funds—are making all sorts of retirement information available in brochure, workbook, and computer formats; employers are taking more time to teach their employees about the importance of utilizing the retirement plans they make available; and articles about retirement appear in magazines and newspapers everywhere.

That's the good news.

The bad news is, in spite of all the written words, the challenge of investing for retirement still rests in your hands. Saving and / or investing for your retirement is an action that you must take. Nobody can really do it for you.

Back to the good news: You can do this. All it takes is learning how to manage money.

Learning how to manage money is a lot like learning how to manage people or horses or kids; it takes time and practice. Once you've been taught the basics (in the case of money management, those basics include the importance of saving money, how compounding interest pays off, and all about the various investment choices available), the most valuable lessons often wind up being the stuff you learn out in the field, through the trial and error of money making.

Because all of our financial needs are different, no one can tell you precisely where to invest to ensure that you'll have the money to live your retirement years in the style in which you've become accustomed today or aspire to live tomorrow. They can only help guide you toward those goals. My research shows that at the bottom of every sizable retirement account or six-figure investment portfolio more often than not lies an individual who has gotten into the very good habit of saving a portion of her or his money.

Habits are behavior patterns we acquire over time. They aren't a part of our gene pool or DNA. They are learned. And because they are learned, anybody can get into the habit of doing almost anything.

If there's one habit worth acquiring that will help us fund our retirement, it's the very practical one of saving money. Saving money can begin with a penny, and if the habit of collecting money continues, that penny can grow into dimes, then dollars. Dollars can then grow into tens, then hundreds. And hundreds of dollars can grow into thousands of them. This saving money business is a lot like that old saying about an acorn: "From a tiny acorn a mighty oak can grow." Think about that the next time you take a walk in the woods. Or add a dollar or two to your retirement accounts.

Glossary

Annuity: An investment product from the insurance industry. Because of the insurance affiliation annuities are contracts offering individuals an opportunity to invest money tax-deferred for a specified period of time. Returns from annuity contracts may be fixed, meaning that the rate of return is specified at the time of purchase, or variable. Annuities typically provide some death benefits to the beneficiaries on these contracts, and they have additional costs and expenses related to them that other kinds of investments don't have. A tax-sheltered annuity is another name for this type of product.

Assets: Anything of value. Someone's personal financial assets might include things like their home and its furnishings, their car, jewelry, collectibles, and investments.

Back-End Load: A sales charge investors pay when they sell some investments. Back-end loads can be found on investment products such as some mutual funds, annuities, and life insurance contracts.

Beneficiary: The person or organization to whom an inheritance passes. Someone can be a beneficiary if, for instance, he is named in a will or is the recipient of the proceeds of a life insurance policy or a retirement plan.

Capital Appreciation (or Loss): Any increase in the value of an asset. Any decrease in value is a capital loss. For mutual fund investors, for instance, if shares of a mutual fund were purchased at $25 per share last year and today the price of one of those shares is $30, the capital appreciation would be 20 percent.

Capital Gain (or Loss): The gain or loss realized when an investment is sold at a price lower than (creating a capital loss) or higher than (creating a capital gain) its original price. Any talk about a capital gain or loss from an investment that hasn't yet been sold refers to only a "paper" loss or gain. An investment has to be sold to realize capital gains or losses.

Compound Interest: Interest that's earned on principal plus the interest that was earned earlier. Compound interest is like money making in perpetual motion; it builds upon itself.

Cost-of-Living Adjustment (COLA): An automatic increase in benefits or salaries paid to someone based upon changes in the consumer price index (CPI).

Defined Benefit Plan (db): A qualified retirement plan that provides specific retirement pension benefits to the employees of the companies offering them. The amount of retirement income employees receive from defined benefit plans is based upon things like how long they have worked for a company, their income level, actuarial analysis, and mathematical formulas.

Defined Contribution Plan (dc): A qualified retirement plan. These are the hot retirement benefit plans of the 1990s. In these programs, the amount of money in someone's actual retirement plan will depend largely upon the amount of contributions made into it and the performance results of the products that person has decided to invest into. The IRS limits the amount of contributions that can be made to defined contribution plans.

Diversification: Diversification is the spreading of money among various kinds of securities and asset classes. For instance, stocks and bonds represent two different kinds of investments from two different asset classes—one, equity; the other, debt. Investing money in stocks and in bonds then would be an example of a diversified portfolio of investments.

Dividend Reinvestment Program (DRIP): A reinvestment program some corporations offer their shareholders. Participating in a DRIP means that all of the dividends received from a stock are used to purchase more shares of it. DRIPs are a convenient way of accumulating more and more shares of a company's stock at little to no extra cost.

Dividends: The payments from the earnings and profits of a corporation that are paid out to a company's shareholders are called dividends. Not all publicly held corporations pay dividends to their shareholders but if they do, the amount of dividend may increase, decrease, or cease to be paid over time.

Dollar Cost Averaging: An investment strategy in which the same amount of money is invested into the same security at regular intervals. By investing in this manner you automatically buy more of a security when its price moves lower and less of it as its price moves higher. As a result, the average cost of that investment can be reduced over time.

Dow Jones Industrial Average (DJIA): An index representing the price-weighted average of 30 stocks actively traded on the New York Stock Exchange. Those stocks currently include AT&T, Allied Signal, Alcoa, American Express, Bethlehem Steel, Boeing, Caterpillar, Chevron, Coca-Cola, Disney, DuPont, Eastman Kodak, Exxon, General Electric, General Motors, Goodyear, IBM, International Paper, McDonald's, Merck, Minnesota Mining and Manufacturing (3M), J. P. Morgan, Philip Morris, Procter & Gamble, Sears, Texaco, Union Carbide, United Technology, Westinghouse, and Woolworth.

Earnings: The profits a company makes after paying all of its expenses, costs, and taxes.

Employee Retirement Income Security Act (ERISA): The name of the 1974 law that sets the standards for the retirement benefits of employees.

Employee Stock Ownership Plans (ESOPs): Qualified retirement plans similar to stock bonus plans. Employees participating in ESOPs have their retirement accounts funded by their employer's stock. How big retirement nest egg ESOPs (or stock bonus plans) grow depends upon whether the per-share value of the stock appreciates (goes up) or depreciates (goes down) and the market conditions during the life of the investment.

Face Value: The value that appears on the face of a bond. Usually represented in $1000 increments. The face value of a bond represents the amount of money one receives when holding a bond until its maturity date. It does not represent the market price of the bond.

Fixed Annuity: An investment contract with an insurance company in which the returns, or interest rates paid to the investors, are stated and identified at the time of purchase.

Fixed-Income Security or Investment: An investment that pays a fixed rate of return. Bonds, like corporate, government, and municipal bonds, are examples of fixed-income securities.

457 Plan: 457s are retirement plans offered to the employees of local, state, and federal governments and not-for-profit organizations.

401(k): 401(k)s are qualified payroll deduction retirement savings plans named after the section of the Tax Code authorizing them. Contributions to a 401(k) plan may be made by employers, employees, or both.

While there are tax advantages for both employers offering and contributing to 401(k)s and employees participating in them, the bottom-line problem with 401(k)s is that employees don't always understand and/or misuse the investment choices and options these retirement plans provide them.

403(b): Named after the section of the Tax Code that authorizes them, this plan is a payroll deduction plan offering participants a tax-deferred retirement savings vehicle similar to the 401(k) plan.

Money available at retirement to someone with a 403(b) plan depends upon how well the employee managed his or her own retirement monies.

Front-End Load: The sales charge on an investment product. In products that carry a front-end load, as some mutual funds do, this sales charge gets paid *before* shares of the fund are purchased.

Guaranteed Investment Contract (GIC): An investment product from the insurance industry representing an obligation of the issuer to pay a specified rate of interest for the full term of the contract and to pay back principal according to a fixed schedule. The payment of principal and interest of GIC contracts are *not* guaranteed by the U.S. government or any other agency. These contracts are referred to as "guaranteed" because of the agreement to pay a fixed rate of return. It is the obligation of the financial institution issuing the GIC to make timely interest and principal payments. The only assurance that an investor has of receiving timely interest and principal payments from a GIC depends upon the financial strength of the insurance company issuing it.

Inflation: A rise in prices due to supply and demand; too much money going after too few goods or services.

Inflation Rate: The percentage change in prices. Inflation rates reflect changes in the consumer price index (CPI) and producer price index (PPI). But inflation is only one side of the story. There is also deflation (the reduction of prices on goods and services) and disinflation (the slowing down of prices).

Inflation Risk: Risk that centers around the future buying power of $1. For example, if inflation were to remain at a constant 3 percent annually, in roughly 24 years it would take $2 to buy what $1 does today.

Individual Retirement Accounts (IRAs): Accounts created to provide individuals a way to save for their retirement. Money invested in IRAs grows tax-deferred until the time it is withdrawn. Contributions into IRAs cannot be more than $2000 per employed individual or $2250 for married couples with a nonworking spouse filing a joint income tax return.

Whether or not an IRA contribution is deducted from one's income tax in the year the contribution is made depends upon one's salary.

Interest: Interest is money a borrower pays to a lender for the use of the lender's money. It can also be the income one receives from a bond, note, certificate of deposit, or from any other debt instrument. Whether you pay or receive interest, it's always stated in percentages—for example, a bond pays 8 percent interest or the bank charges me 9 percent for my car loan.

Keogh Plans: Qualified retirement plans for the self-employed that can be established either as defined contribution or defined benefit plans. The self-employed and full- or part-time individuals may open this kind of retirement account. The IRS sets the limits for annual contributions.

Liabilities: Debts. Any money owned to someone or to an institution is considered a liability.

Liquidity Risk: An investment risk revolving around how quickly an investment can be sold and the money from it recouped.

Load: Another name for a sales charge. These sales charges may be paid at various times. Two of the most popular loads are front-end loads, sales charges paid prior to making the investment, and back-end loads, sales charges paid when selling the investment. Sales charges are the means in which commission-based salespeople earn their livings.

Low Load: A sales charge on an investment, like a mutual fund, considered by industry standards to be low. An example of a low-load fund within the mutual fund industry would be a fund with a sales charge of 3 percent.

Money-Market Fund: A mutual fund investing into short-maturing securities. Such products come in two forms: money-market deposit accounts (MMDAs), which are money-market funds that are available at banks in which the monies invested in them may be FDIC-insured if the bank carries that insurance; and money-market mutual funds (MMMFs), which are money-market mutual funds sold through mutual fund families that are not federally insured.

Money Purchase Plans: Defined contribution retirement plans in which the employer contributes a fixed percentage of compensation into their employees' retirement accounts.

Mutual Fund: An investment company that pools money from its shareholders and invests that money into a variety of vehicles including stocks, bonds, and money-market instruments. Monies invested into mutual funds are professionally managed and each fund has a specific investment objective such as "long-term growth" or "current income." Individuals selling mutual funds need a license to do so.

Net Asset Value (NAV): The per-share price of a mutual fund. NAVs are computed daily and represent the market worth of a mutual fund's total assets, minus liabilities, divided by the total number of shares outstanding in the fund.

Net Assets: The bottom line. Subtracting all debts from all assets equals the net assets.

No-Load: An investment product that has no sales charge.

Nonqualified Annuity: An annuity that's purchased with after-tax monies, that is, money that you've already paid taxes on.

Nonqualified Retirement Plan: A retirement plan that offers no special tax treatment for the monies initially used to fund it. In other words, taxes have already been paid on the money put into these plans.

Objective: The reason for creating an investment product or making an investment. Another way of looking at an objective might be to ask, What's the point? Investment products, like mutual funds, have investment objectives just as people do. Examples of mutual fund objectives include capital appreciation or income or growth and income. Wise investors match up an investment product's objective with their own.

Portfolio: All the securities owned by an individual or an institution. Someone's retirement portfolio might consist of such things as individual stocks, bonds, and CDs.

Profit-Sharing Plan: A retirement plan in which an employer may contribute a percentage of the company's profits to a retirement plan for its employees, allowing them to share in the profits of the company.

Prospectus: A document that contains detailed information about an investment product. A prospectus outlines the reason an investment product was created and points out the particulars of it. It includes what the objective of the product is, who is managing it, where and how the money invested in it will be spent, how to buy and sell shares of the investment, what the sales charges are, and a host of other valuable information.

Qualified Retirement Plans: Qualified retirement plans are those with tax advantages for both the employer offering them and the employee participating in them.

Employers making contributions into qualified plans are allowed to deduct those contributions in the year they are made. For employees, any contributions made into qualified retirement plans are not taxed until distributions are taken out.

Risk: The chance each and every one of us makes when we decide to invest our money. The "chance" is that we may or may not get back the original amount of money invested. Our investment returns may be greater than, equal to, or lesser than the original amount of money invested. Risk is an ever-present part of investing.

Risk Tolerance: The ability to handle the fact that invested money may fluctuate in value. Those who do not want their principal to decrease in value would have no investment risk tolerance. Others with a greater risk tolerance level don't mind their principal going up and down in value.

Section 457 Plan: A deferred compensation plan into which both the participants of the plan and their employers may contribute. A 457 plan is usually offered to an employee of a state government, a subdivision of a state government, or a not-for-profit organization.

Simplified Employee Pension (SEP): A retirement plan for the self-employed or small-company owners allowing them to invest a percentage of their pretax dollars into this qualified retirement plan. SEPs are considered the most basic type of defined contribution plan in existence and were established to provide small-company owners and the self-employed with an inexpensive retirement plan.

Standard & Poor's 500: A stock index measuring the changes in the 500 stocks making up this composite.

Stock: Also referred to as an equity, a stock represents ownership in a corporation.

Tax-Deferred: Taxes due at a later date.

Tax-Exempt: The interest earned from tax-exempt investment products is exempt from state, local, and federal taxes.

Time Horizon: How long you intend on keeping your money invested. For example, if you began saving for retirement when you were 35, and planned on retiring at age 65, your investment time horizon would be 30 years.

Total Return: A combination of the change in the per-share price of an investment plus any income received from dividends and capital gains.

Tax-Sheltered Annuities (TSAs): Also referred to as tax-deferred annuities (TDAs) or Section 403(b) plans because they are governed by Internal Revenue Code Section 403(b), these retirement programs are available only to employees of nonprofit organizations and employees of public school systems. To invest in TSAs, employees use a salary reduction plan.

Variable Annuity: Variable annuities are mutual funds with an insurance contract wrapper around them. Unlike fixed annuities in which the returns are stated in variable annuities, the returns will fluctuate.

Vesting: Your right to receive a portion or all of the proceeds in a retirement plan. Vesting guidelines must follow the rules of ERISA, vary from employer to employer, and are based upon your years of service to your employer. There are two types of vesting time tables: *cliff* and *gradual*. In *cliff* vesting, employees become 100 percent vested after working a set number of years. *Gradual* vesting happens in stages. For instance, someone participating in a retirement program in which *gradual* vesting is a part might be privy to 5% of the contributions during their first year of service to the company; 20% after two years of employment; 30% after three years, etc., until a specified number of years have passed and the employee becomes 100% vested in the employer's retirement plan. The money you personally contribute to your 401(k) or 403(b) plans, however, is automatically 100% vested from day one.

Yield: The income, from interest or dividends, received from an investment and expressed as an annualized percentage rate.

Index

About the Author

Dian Vujovich is a freelance business writer whose weekly column about mutual funds is featured in *The Miami Herald* and is nationally syndicated by Newspaper Enterprise Association. She also writes on business and financial matters for a wide array of periodicals; conducts educational financial seminars for various groups, organizations, and corporations; and is the author of *Straight Talk about Mutual Funds*.